My Now for the
Single Parent

Moovin4ward Publishing
Huntsville, Alabama

Copyright 2014 Moovin4ward Publishing

Library of Congress Control Number: 2014910229

ISBN: Paperback   978-0-9910227-24

Printed in the United States of America

All rights reserved. No part of this publication may be reproduced, stored in a retrieval system or transmitted in any form or by any means, electronic, mechanical, photocopying, recording or otherwise, without the written permission of the publisher.

Publisher:
   Moovin4ward Publishing
   A Division of Moovin4ward Presentations LLC
   www.Moovin4ward.com

Contents

Part 1: Temporary Setback 7

There Are Blessings in the Broken 9
Happiness in Divorce... 17
Staying Strong During the Storm... 33
Where Are My Notes?.. 41
But My God.. 69

Part 2: Back on Track 77

Deferred, Not Denied: How to Get Your Dreams Back on Track 79
A Lesson from an Octopus... 91
The Me Time Principle 99
Taking the Sin out of SINGLE 121
Learn to Invest in Your Child's Success 133

Part 3: World's Greatest 139

We Can't Be Married... But Let's Be Good Parents 141
Divorced... But Still a Dad 155
Show Unconditional Love 169
Full Sun for Balance 177
School on Your Time, Not Theirs 189

My Now…

...for the Single Parent

Part 1: Temporary Setback

My Now...

Elethia Gay

Elethia Gay is an experienced life coach, author, speaker and personal trainer. After receiving her MBA from Mercer University, she completed extensive training in personal life management and organizational behavior. Her areas of expertise include: Diversity and Inclusion, The Whole Brain model, 7 Habits of Highly Effective People, Managerial Skills, Effective Communication Skills and Color Analysis. Elethia's expertise in brand management allowed her to build over 10 years of marketing and advertising experience with brands like Domino's Pizza and Ford. She took that branding expertise to her personal clients and helps them reinvent their brand through personalized image strategies. Her personal branding techniques focus on mind and body because she believes your personal brand is more than what you see. In 2008, she began a national speaking career that has enabled her to share her expertise with over 10,000 students each year. In her personal time, she serves as a Bullying Prevention Trainer with NCCY.org. Elethia also enjoys teaching fitness classes, designing for her new t-shirt line, and serving on grass root campaigns that promote economic independence for women.

F: facebook.com/alexanderqimagegroup
T: @aqimagegroup
W: aqimagegroup.com
E: info@aqimagegroup.com

...for the Single Parent

There Are Blessings in the Broken
Elethia Gay

I know this piece does not focus much on divorce. "Divorced" is not who I am today. When someone asks me if I am single I answer "yes," not "divorced." For me, this is a time of rebuilding. In the last three years I have had a chance to travel extensively. I became a fitness instructor and personal trainer. I am rebuilding my personal branding business and coming out of this darn cocoon. At first I thought, "Now I get to create the blueprint and set the foundation." However, in creating the plan, choosing the materials, and laying the foundation, I realized the plan was already in place, the foundation was set and it was up to me to trust and move on cue. That became clearer as I grew closer in my relationship with the Lord.

The Lord of it all has only my best interest. The Lord's plan is greater than I could have ever imagined for myself. Yes, I like to make moves. Yes, I'm still learning the meaning of standing still. However, in prayer I receive my instructions and in faith I have found my next step. What's life after divorce like? I have a list of goals. Instead of pulling out credit cards and working crazy hours to make them happen, I pray and trust in the Lord –

something I didn't do in the past. Earlier I mentioned who I am not but most importantly is WHOSE I AM... a child of God, a daughter, a mom and even stronger both mentally and physically. With that in my heart, I will continue to thrive.

Below is a letter I wrote to my brother right before he was married. I never gave it to him. However I found it during a case of writer's block and wanted to use it. Not only is it a letter to my brother but also words to my child.

Dear Brother,

Normally I would not congratulate one this way; however, you are my brother and I love you too much not to. Marriage is such a wonderful thing. You wake up to your best friend for the rest of your life. You will laugh together, cry together and experience life's great joys and journeys… together!

Before getting married, I thought being in love was all you needed. No shared goals or mentoring. Maybe a little prayer but, to me, it was all based on my definition of love. I was 25 and so unaware of life's peaks and valleys. However, in those valleys I learned my I AM; I am a child of God. Once you realize the power in this revelation and truth, I can promise that all you do will eventually work out for the greater good.

The ring, the ceremony, the vows are just part of the process. It was on my journey through the peaks and the valleys that I truly learned about marriage, myself and life...

Truth is Truth

Truth is not what you think others need to hear. I have come to know Truth as the Divine and I have learned to call this Truth at all times. Earlier in life, I would seek the advice of others much before going to God. In seeking their advice or even approval, I would leave certain pieces of information out. I was ashamed, fearful or not interested in hearing their truth. Yet, how can you receive the advice you so desperately need from a person who has a limited view of who you are? Then I realized I was making this way too hard. From my victories to my mistakes, the Lord knew exactly what I was going to do before it was done. Before I uttered a word or took a step, the Lord knew where I was going. If the Lord only wants the best for me, then even with my mistakes, I could still turn to the Lord. Don't get me wrong, one can definitely learn from sharing with others. Yet the Lord knew the truth, the whole truth and nothing but the truth. Thus, even in my mistakes, I could go to him for guidance. Storms will come and you might even stumble... even on the path to his promise; however, take it to the Lord, dust yourself off and get back on that path.

Truth is not what the wisest person in the family has to say. It knows what God has for you is for you. Whatever may come in your marriage, in your family or in your career - you cannot abandon the wonderful outcome at the end of each journey if you put God first. Come what may in your life, don't give up. Dust yourself off, stay focused on the Lord's promises through the word and walk in His truth.

Continue to Grow

I am not sure who began the rumor that you need someone or something to complete you. There is only one you. You will not find another 35%, 47% or 10% of you out there. Your purpose for being here is not for someone else to make you whole. You grow and become stronger by continuously feeding your mind, body and soul, then lovingly feeding those around you. However you cannot complete them either. You can only be part of their evolvement and path to fulfillment.

Never stop learning to be a better man, son, husband, father, human being, etc. Never stop learning. When you stop learning, you stop growing. Think about it. The Lord wants us to increase. The only way to do that is to feed on something. Feed on his word. Feed on his promises. Learn it, apply it and live it so that you add more and more to who you are. Where am I going with all this? When the loving becomes routine, when the hips start spreading (both male and female), work is just a job, and the kids are in your ear, where do you find understanding and strength? Well, you read the bible. You read *A Course in Miracles*, *The Five Love Languages*, *Think and Grow Rich, The Richest Man in Babylon,* Sara Young, Max Lucado, TD Jakes, Wayne Dyer, etc. It may also include Baby Einstein, PBS Kids, or Sesame Street. Even with tools meant to help our children grow, we can learn something new.

Life is a Journey

Life is a trip with many plans, blueprints and goals. Whether you use a blackberry, iPhone, android or black book, our lives are constantly ablaze with our next appointment or meeting. You can set goals in life. You can even work towards them. Yet, you must understand that there may be times the appointment may change or cancelled altogether. The car may not start; dinner may not be what you expected; or the baby may have a little surprise in his diaper right before you pull off to the sitter. The plan doesn't always unfold so neatly. The bottom line is no matter where you set the desired destination, the true joy in life is in the present. It is in the bumpy, messy and often funny present. Learn something from anything. Be present and enjoy the ride. Your best times are not what you plan and wait for… your best times are now!

Love always,

Big Sis

Maybe later I can give a more technical view on divorce like how to adjust your budget, find a good lawyer, file taxes and handle custody agreements. Right now, I am not there. I am single and living Truth. I didn't understand whose I was. I thought marriage, people and things would help reveal life's purpose. Now I know my truth is within me. Now I know you have to feed into your mate; sow seeds of Divine nourishment like forgiveness, understanding and patience into the relationship. Marriage is helping each other grow. You grow together in the day to day. Help your spouse and ask your spouse for help. If he/she cleans all the time, then pick up a broom. If you make dinner all the time, try cooking together. Never take him/her for granted. Remember he/she feeds into you. You are a unit.

One more thing... The person you are blessed with could have been granted to someone else, yet they are with you. That alone is worth daily appreciation and maybe a Gucci every year (kidding). What I am asking is, don't just tell them. Show them.

Coming from a single parent household, I had little patience in being submissive or submitting completely to a man. Yet, I ask, "Should not a married man be God's example of a great husband, dad and leader to his family?" While taking the lead is both empowering and exhausting, do it with love as your guide. Show your family that love is not vulnerability. Show your family that seeking guidance is not vulnerability. Show them, don't just tell them.

Should not a married woman exemplify God's qualities as a wife, mom, and person of hope and support to the family? From what I have learned, hope requires trust, another challenge to the independent. Yet when you know your truth, you can trust in His plan. Then your ability to support your family comes in the form of the hope they see in you!

Wherever you are in life - married, engaged or dealing with some other big transition - stay the course. Know whose you are and that He is your truth. When you pray for direction, pray for the tools you need to heal and grow. Also, understand that life is a journey. Be present even in the toughest times. I chose to end my marriage after prayer and heavy meditation. But I had to be present for the answer to become clear. Finally, pray every day because in all things prayer changes things!

My Now…

Adebayo O. Adegun

Adebayo "Make My 'Mpact" Adegun is an IT Consultant, Trainer, Speaker, Counselor, Visionary and Author. He's always enthusiastic about helping people to be productive. He has written both published and unpublished articles to help people and organizations to be productive, he is also one of the featured authors of the book, My NOW for the College Grad.

He holds a BSc. Degree in Technology, a Master's Degree in ICT, a Diploma in Educational Psychology and a Diploma in Business, Management and Entrepreneurship. In addition, he holds various certifications in IT and Management. And has worked and consulted for numerous multinational organizations.

Recently, he became a Licensed PSSP Consultant at Moovin4ward Presentations, USA for Africa; a top motivational company aimed at empowering youth.

Adebayo is the Founder and President of CrossTie Solutions, an organization aimed at improving Productivity and Professionalism of Individuals and Businesses in Africa.

www.crosstiesolutions.com
makemympact@crosstiesolutions.com
@makemympact

...for the Single Parent

Happiness in Divorce
Adebayo O. Adegun

What are you saying right now! Could this title be real? Can I ever be happy in divorce? Yes! Yes! Yes! You can still be on cloud nine in divorce. But before we go into how to achieve that, let's discuss the rudiments of this woeful situation called "Divorce".

WHAT IS DIVORCE?

I feel completely downhearted whenever I watch TV programs, listen to radio programs, read magazines or follow a gist on social media about a union God has ordained being torn asunder. I ask myself why divorce again? Is that the last option? When will these problems stop? When will couples live together and forever like Eldorado? Before I take it further, let's discuss what divorce really is.

"Divorce, or dissolution, as it is increasingly becoming known, is a legislatively created, judicially administered process that legally terminates a marriage no longer considered viable by one or both of the spouses, and that permits both to remarry". – Microsoft Encarta. Statistics have shown that about 40% of marriages in various nations today end in divorce. Among Roman Catholics throughout the world, the traditional attitude is that a true marriage (one entered into as a religious sacrament) is indissoluble by legal means. Notwithstanding this strict interdiction of divorce, many Roman Catholics procure divorces in the courts. The Roman Catholic Church views such divorces as merely a form of legal separation, and remarriage is not permitted.

CAUSES OF DIVORCE

From the miniature research I did recently, I want to share with you some causes of this extremely distressing experience called "Divorce". The result shows that majority of the causes of divorce had surfaced during their relationship or courtship, but they tend to manage it hoping those attitudes and problems of their partners will change with patience and time. I asked some single parents recently why they divorced, and the responses were "I couldn't cope ANYMORE with my spouses' attitudes and problems". I questioned further "'ANYMORE'? You mean you knew about those attitudes and problems during your relationship?" and the responses were "YES". Then why did you decide to go to the altar with him or her? They said, "We thought there would be a change", I exhaled. These people forgot that the transformation of a man's attitudes and problems are not through their effort but from God and the person involved. I'm sharing this with you because I don't want the single ladies and men out there to make such mistakes again. I'm concerned about your being happy in your marriages because that's when you can become productive, which is my VISION in life – improving productivity and professionalism of individuals and businesses.

What pressures are you currently facing that will make you settle for just anybody? I tell most solemnly, you will rush out from a marriage you were pressured into by either your friends or your family. Ask yourself this question during relationship or courtship "If I don't marry this man or woman, who else?" If your response is "No one", that's what I call "LOVE" but if your response is "I wish it's <u>that</u> man or woman", kindly walk away. And if you don't do that now, you will eventually do it when you later meet that person you wished you had. Would you rather be in a peaceful state of mind as a single and wait for the right and just person to come than to be in a marriage where you are perplexed each day of your life with the miserable attitudes and problems of your spouse? "I came not into this realm as merchandise, nor yet to be married to any merchant" - Catherine of Aragón (1485 - 1536). Can you pick up a pen now and write according to priorities all you want in your spouse? Most partners omitted this valuable period of their lives. That's why when the right person comes, they are shown the red card because they never had the idea of what they really want. I'm sure you don't want to make such mistakes too. Try this and I promise you "The Law of Attraction" will bring to you exactly what you desire. Be mindful that you might not get 100% of what you wrote, but when you see 70% in that person, go grab it!

Women are called troublemakers, is that really true? Ask yourself and respond sincerely? Studies have shown that 80% of divorce court cases today are initiated by women. "Now one of the greatest reasons why so many husbands and wives make shipwreck of their lives together is because a man is always seeking happiness, while a woman is on a perpetual still hunt for trouble - Dorothy Dix (1861 - 1951) U.S. journalist and writer". If a man is the head of the home, then a woman should be the heart. Apparently without the heart, the head can't function and that's why I feel women should be at the side of making peace when there are issues with their partners. Men with ego will always fall victim of divorce because they feel reluctant to say "sorry" when they do something unjust. Apology doesn't mean that you were wrong, or the other person was right, it means that your relationship is valuable than your ego. Men! Can we just take that ego out of our lives, while women should not push a man to the wall rather be the peacemaker? "Before you marry a person you should first make them use a computer with a slow internet connection to see how truly they can cope with frustration" – Whitney Cummings.

Sincerely, if I don't talk about adultery as the most common cause of separation in marriages today, this article is not complete. The big question is when and why does adultery come into a man or a woman's life? The only answer is CONTENMENT! In most cases, especially in relationships and marriages, you will only get 75% of what you NEED and you will hardly get the other 25% that you WANT in your relationship. There is always another person (man or woman) that you will meet and that will readily offer you the 25% which is lacking in your relationship or marriage that you WANT. And believe me, 25% looks really good when you are not getting it at all in your current relationship or marriage. But the problem is that you are lured to leave the good 75% that you have already and really NEED, for the 25% that you WANT thinking that you will get something better. Be careful in deciding between what you WANT and NEED in your life. Adultery happens when you start looking for what you don't have. Wow! This colleague of mine is so caring, intelligent, tender and considerate…qualities my spouse does not possess.

Along the path of life, you will find a woman or a man who will be more charming, sensitive, more alluring, more thoughtful, richer, have a greater sex appeal, etc. And you will find a woman or man who will need you and go crazy over you more than your spouse ever did. Be not deceived, for that is the law of nature that applies to new things. Remember no wife or husband is perfect. Don't say because your wife is a housewife, who doesn't work and is always on slippers and pajamas, smelling of onions, garlic and fish oil, you went ahead and fell for a young sales representative that visits your office in sharp black suit, high heels, a red pencil-out skirt with inviting fragrance; or because your husband is the quiet type, not sexually skillful and a workaholic, you get interested in discussions involving how a friendly colleague who is still single gives treat to his concubines with much energetic sexual satisfaction. You might only get 75% of what you are looking for in your spouse. And when you start searching for the missing 25% in your husband or wife, adultery knocks. Remember what I said earlier, if you had written what you want in your spouse, I don't think the 25% is worth an issue between you two.

Wait a minute! That's only 25% of what you want but don't have. Don't throw away the 75% that you already have! Remember the years you have been with each other, the problems you went through together, the notable moments of joy and sadness as a couple, the many adjustments you have made to accept and love each other, the loads of memories that you have accumulated as lovers and everything else.

Adultery happens when you start looking for what you don't have. But faithfulness happens when you start thanking God for what you have already. The purpose of laying more emphasis on adultery is that I want you to start appreciating what you have right now and stop asking for trouble by desiring what your neighbor has. Remember trouble usually comes disguised.

EFFECT OF DIVORCE

When you fail to adhere and turn over a new leaf to my latter causes of divorce, you are welcoming problems into your relationship or marriage. It is a pity that the children are always the worst beneficiaries of these conflicts. Let's discuss the impact of divorce on the children as they are my utmost concern. When a marriage ends in divorce, all the individuals connected to the relationship are affected. Perhaps none of them is so affected as the children because of their innocence and immaturity, children won't be able to accommodate the stress as adults will. Their reactions and behavior can be dangerous. Children are particularly vulnerable to the effects of divorce. Unable to understand and process such complex matters of life, children resort to alternative ways of expressing their heartache and confusion. The fact is that the divorce of parents remains with children, to some degree, all of their lives. If only couples can foresee the impact of divorce on their children, I'm sure they will devote time, energy, patience to work things out to avert the ugly monster.

Faber and Wittenborn (2010) report that on average, children in divorced families and stepfamilies, as compared to those in non-divorced families, are more likely to exhibit behavioral and emotional problems, lower social competence and self-esteem, less socially responsible behavior, and poorer academic achievement. Some other harrowing elements of divorce for children are the constant change of their surroundings and the lack of control. Not only is there a change in who they live with, but most often there is a change in where they live and the duration of time spent at each location. After all said, I am sure you don't want your innocent children to go through this rigorous period in their lives. Do you?

SHARING PERSONAL EXPERIENCE

I met Hannah at a "Leadership Program" I co-facilitated recently. She confronted me after the programme and booked an appointment with me to hear her pathetic story. This is her story;

My name is Dr. Hannah, and I am a child of divorce. My parents began their divorce when I was 15 years.

On the good side of my story, I finished from secondary school with straight A's, got into a top university to study medicine, completed my medical school program, finished with a first class honors, went for "housemanship" and did my NYSC, got a job, got engaged, got married and moved

My Now...

from Abeokuta, Ogun State Nigeria to Lagos Island, Lagos State, Nigeria where I've finally found the peace and stability I've longed for. I live with my husband and our lovely kid, and I work in one of the top-class hospitals on Lagos Island. I am a successful person today because I am happy, fulfilled and satisfied. How, you may wonder, did I survive all the chaos and now consider myself to be over the moon?

First, let me take you back to the terrible day when my parents told us their marriage was over. I was 15, my brother, 11 and a younger sister, 9. We were in SSS1, JSS2 and Primary 4 classes respectively at a boarding school when they made the decision to divorce. But I knew something was happening, because our parents would always come visiting on separate days, while other children have both parents visiting at the same time. And when I asked any of one of my parents why the other was not there, it's always the excuse of business trips and very busy schedules. Their responses were always short and suspicious. When we arrived home from school for the session break, my first instinct was to check my mom's room, because I knew I would find it empty. I asked my dad about my mom's belongings and he kept mum. He said we would talk about it later.

Three days later, my mom came and I asked her where she had been. She started crying and just said, "I don't live here anymore." I just burst out tears which was enough to break a 15-year-old girl's heart.

Psychologically, it was extremely hard for me to complement both my education and parents' divorce for the next two years to complete my secondary school. Nevertheless, I made eight A's and scored above 300 in my UTM Examination which was more than enough to study any course in any university. I got admission to study medicine. I lived my life out of a mystery but I was determined never to let the issue affect my academic performance. First, I lived with my mom but we fought constantly so I moved in with my dad at the end of my first year. I moved back in with mom at the end of my third year, then back in with dad right before graduation. But most of the time, I stayed at my best friend's house. Her parents were going through an ugly divorce, too, and we were able to console each other.

My parents' divorce was antagonistic. Many at times, they put me in the middle, used me as the messenger or criticized each other in front of me whenever they have to meet over our welfare. These deleterious experiences are

My Now...

part of my past, but they shaped my present life in many positive ways. Remember at the beginning of my story when I said I was successful? I am. I think it's because my parents' struggles forced me to grow up faster, pushed me away from their problems and into books and studies. I learned to cope, to grow strong, and to believe in myself instead of joining in their drama and becoming a victim. But not everyone was that lucky.

How did I do it, you want to ask now? I learned to lean on close friends, and these friends became the family I needed at the time. I learned to be open to relationships. To be candid with you, I never thought my marriage would send down blessings on me. I thought I would fail at marriage just as my parents did. I was afraid because of numerous studies which say children of divorce have a higher risk of getting divorced. But when I met my husband, also a child of divorce, none of those fears came into reality. I told myself I wasn't my parents and I didn't have to make their mistakes. My relationship was not theirs - I don't hold grudges, I communicate my feelings, never go to bed angry and had an open mind - all the things my parents were never good at.

In spite of all the pain they caused, one day we should learn to see our parents as the young people they once were, starting a marriage with hopes and dreams to raise wonderful children. We look at their early photos and feel sadness for them. Most parents will intentionally not hurt their children. But when it happens, the children become the most affected.

Lastly, about two years ago, my mom and dad placed a call through to me and my siblings apologizing for messing up a part of our childhood, for not handling things the way they should have. I know they had regrets. After all was said, I thanked them and told them how much I loved them because I've turned things around for good and that has made me who I am today.

Whao! That was all I said at that point and promised to publish her story to motivate someone out there. She was so glad to hear that – a source of inspiration to others.

HAPPINESS OF THE HEART, SELF FULFILLMENT AND SELF SATISFACTION IN DIVORCE

As a psychologist, motivational speaker, and visionary, I'm so much passionate about you being productive in whatever you do. There are no doubts some dreams and visions have been killed because of this emotional disorder. Only a happy mind can be productive. Are you the innocent child, the divorce or the divorcee, I can quite feel what you are going through at the moment which might be depriving you from reaching the peak. Here are some quotes I've got for you. Enjoy!

GET INSPIRED BY THESE QUOTES!

"Take your mind out of every now and then and dance on it. It is getting all caked up." That was his way of saying, "Try something new, break new ground, and get out of your rut." – Mark Twain

"There is nothing either good or bad, but thinking makes it so." - Shakespeare

"It's not the mountain we conquer, but ourselves. – Edmund Hillary (First to climb Mt. Everest)

"Ninety-nine percent of failures come from people who have the habit of making excuses." – George Washington Carver

"Our strength is seen in the things we stand for; our weakness is seen in the things we fall for." – Theodore Epp

"A difficult crisis can be more readily endured if we retain the conviction that our existence holds a purpose – a cause to pursue, a person to love, a goal to achieve". – John C. Maxwell

"A determined person is one who, when they get to the end of their rope, ties a knot and hangs on." – Joe L. Griffith

"One who gains strength by overcoming obstacles possesses the only strength which can overcome adversity." – Albert Schweitzer

"Circumstances do not make you what you are… they reveal what you are." - John C. Maxwell

"Doggedness in Divorce accomplishes your potentials" – Adebayo O. Adegun

As much as I would advise you do not suffer in silence, it is pleasurable conquering the fears in your relationship now, so that you stay hooked and live happily ever after. Life is beautiful!

Tina L. Collazo

Tina L. Collazo is a mother, poet, writer, speaker, and entrepreneur. Over the past 5 years, single parents have sought out her wisdom about how to have success in their life spiritually, mentally, emotionally, physically, relationally, and financially.

Tina has written a devotional called "Virgin to The Mic" filled with uplifting and inspiring poems as a result of her journey as a divorcee and single mom. She serves as a Life Group Leader for Single Mothers and Separated/Divorced Women as well as an AWANA Leader for the First Graders. Tina has been invited as a guest speaker at local high schools to talk about Marketing, Business Office Environment, and launching "Success for Teens, Teens Using the Slight Edge".

Tina is a mother of two awesome boys, J.C. and Nicolaus. She is a successful Real Estate Agent and Investor, and specializes in the Northern Virginia market.

Email: tina@tinacollazo.com
Website: www.TinaCollazo.com
Twitter: @TinaCollazo

...for the Single Parent

Staying Strong During the Storm
Tina L. Collazo

A divorce is never easy for the parent or for the child. As a single parent, you have to be stay strong for your kids. They need to see strength in you and you have to keep the right frame of mind.

I remember losing my mind when I left my ex-husband and joined the ranks of being a single parent. I was hurt that I had to leave him because our marriage was unhealthy and abusive. Many people don't talk about abuse nor how to identify it. Little did I know I was in a verbally, mentally, emotionally, and headed into a physically abusive relationship with my children's father. It wasn't like that happened overnight. Since my ex-husband refused to get marriage counseling, I started getting counseling for myself. This is how I realized that my childhood impacted my relationship with my husband. Obviously, it takes two for things not work, but that experience helped me work on me and identify my issues. My dysfunctional behavior from the inability to effectively communicate to shutting down was a result of my childhood experience with my parents and what they would say to me. For example, if I didn't like what I was experiencing with people, I would cut them off emotionally and detach myself. Overall, life sent me dysfunctional messages and relationships that ultimately caused my marriage to fall apart.

After a couple months of depression from the initial separation, I finally got it together. I had to get my mind right and feed it with hope when I didn't see a way out. I read so many inspirational books about spirituality and finances, specifically. TD Jakes became one of my favorite authors that fed my spirit. His books "Water in the Wilderness" and "Repositioning Your Life Without Limits" helped propel me forward. Dave Ramsey's book, "The Total Money Makeover," helped open my eyes about how I had mismanaged my finances and the steps I needed to take to become financially free. These books gave me hope.

Something else I noticed during that time when my sons, J.C. and Nicolaus, were very little was that they would act out how I felt. I would be cool as cucumber on the outside, and freaking out on the inside about all the drama I was experiencing in my life. They would cut up and act out when I was at my worst emotionally. I had to accept that they were a reflection of me. I didn't like what I was seeing. My breakthrough came when the light bulb turned on and I realized I had to make a choice. I could stay depressed and stay in that bad place or make a decision to get strong and rebuild my life. I chose to be strong and move forward. I reminded myself that I had it going on before I got married. Now it's just Tina plus 2. I can do it again!

...for the Single Parent

What helped me move forward was my faith in God. I got saved right before I graduated from college. I was that girl who would go to school, go to work to pay for school, hit the clubs with my girls Thursday through Sunday morning, and show up at church on Sunday crying because I wanted to give my life to Christ, but didn't want to change. On December 5, 1999, I gave my life to Christ and about 3 months later I met their father who wasn't saved. As a baby in Christ, I struggled with sex before marriage while we were dating. I actually got pregnant after the third year of our relationship and married him several months later before my first son was born. I knew I shouldn't have said yes to his proposal, but I did it anyway because I felt obligated. Looking back in hindsight, I believe he asked me because he was trying to do the right thing even though he wasn't ready to be a husband or a father. It was actually becoming a mom for the first time that opened my eyes to how our relationship was so wrong. By 2005, my youngest son, Nicolaus, was born and it was definitely downhill from there. In the meantime, I started getting stronger in my faith in 2006 because I knew Jesus was the only person that could help deliver me from the living hell I was experiencing in my marriage. By 2007, I left my ex-husband and joined a new church to build my life a solid foundation this time. The mistake we made in our relationship was that we didn't put God first, and it fell apart when life happened and I never wanted to experience that again. At this new church I started growing by going to Sunday service, then Wednesday night Bible Study, and then ultimately joining the Evangelism Ministry and learning that I had a spiritual gift. From 2008 to 2012, I was able to build my spiritual foundation on a solid rock at this church. I became sold out for Christ. In addition, every area of my life changed for the better and I became stronger.

By early 2012, God transitioned me once again to another church and He revealed to me that He wanted to take me to the next level in my relationship with Him. Over the past 2 years, I've changed so much that I don't recognize myself. I came seeking how I can move into my God-given purpose and bless others. Now I'm a Life Group Leader for this church for Single Mothers and Separated/Divorced Women as well as an AWANA (Approved Workmen Are Not Ashamed) Leader for First Graders. I can't believe how my life has changed and how I'm fulfilling my destiny everyday. I'm living on purpose now, and my passion is to empower single parents and divorcees who are walking down the path I've already been.

I've learned to become strong for my children. I focus on having a balanced life spiritually, mentally, emotionally, physically, and financially. I've never neglected my kids in such a way that they felt abandoned by me. If anything, I have had the "I got to do what I need to do" attitude. My goal has been to be consistent and stable in their lives. I wanted them to know how much I love them and that I was their rock. I always envisioned J.C. and Nic giving their "Momma Shout Out" when they get older and became someone great. As a single parent, we make so many sacrifices for our children and feel guilty that we can't give them everything we want. Funny enough, we give them what they need and why can't that be good enough? I work hard to show my children love by what I say and do. So in my head, I hear their speeches going a little something like this, "I want to thank my mom for being there and encouraging me and speaking life into me when I didn't believe in myself and for showing me that nurturing relationships are a great gift." I can't wait until that day because I know in my heart that the blood, sweat, and tears that I experienced yesterday and today will pay off tomorrow. It's only a matter of time.

By God's grace, I have managed to keep it together despite everything that I've been through. I feed my mind all the time with good information whether it's reading a thought-provoking book, listening to a motivational message, or watching something inspirational that will change my life in a powerful way. I once read that the books you read today will impact who you become 5 years from now. I'm seeing some of the fruit from that philosophy in my life right now. These strategies are also helpful when I'm feeling depressed, discouraged, or afraid of something going on in my life.

My father recently shared with me about a friend of his whose daughter was separated and going through a divorce. She and her kids moved in with his friend. The daughter became so depressed that she stopped working, and her mother ended up providing for all of them and taking care of her kids. My advice to the daughter would be, "Sister, you have to get your emotions together and your mind right. You have to make yourself #1 and not feel guilty about that. When you're strong, everybody benefits and becomes strong. Don't take your family for granted just because they can or want to help you. Figure out how to help yourself first. When you can't find the strength to get back on your feet for yourself, do it for your kids." That's what I did and I have no problem doing what I need to do for my children. Over the years, I've encouraged other single parents to do the same so they can move forward and out of the rut they are in.

My parents moved to Florida by the time I went through my divorce and became a single parent. I couldn't get to them without going on a three hour plane ride or driving almost 24 hours by car. Bottom-line, I had to learn how to survive as a single mom on my own. However, I'm grateful for the month long summer vacations for the kids in Florida while I stayed in Virginia to work, and all the emotional support and words of encouragement they gave me since they couldn't physically be here. Also, I'm thankful for the spiritual family that helped me with my kids since I didn't have any family close by. Although being a single parent has had its ups and downs, the journey has been well worth it to see my children happy and have the peace and joy I experience everyday.

...for the Single Parent

I didn't know how strong I was until it happened.

My Now…

...for the Single Parent

Where Are My Notes?
Anonymous

"Alisha, I need you to turn around now and come back! I need the folder that I left in your car. It was by my feet. Oh my God! I'm texting you right now."

You hit the end button on your phone and maneuver to the keyboard.

You furiously text:

Please come back! I left my folder in your car. It has my notes for this presentation. On in 24 minutes. YIKES! Hurry!

Hitting the send button, your mind races as you recall your morning.

Old Yella, your 15 year-old, yellow Land Rover had been squealing all week and decided not to wake up today. Facing a brutal winter morning in the Midwest, you opened the hood, put the stick in the top and amateurishly inspected your car.

"Hmmm," you said to yourself, adjusting the gloves you snagged during the after-Christmas sale at Target. "Just as I suspected...a bunch of metal covered in black stuff."

Slamming the hood, a sigh broke free from your lips.

You had to figure out how to get your car fixed. Preferably before Monday's big meeting downtown. But where could you find a mechanic, on a Saturday evening or Sunday to fix this car?

At that moment, your phone rang. It was Alisha calling to brag about her big date with Geoff last night. She was on her way to breakfast at Lou's Diner, your hometown's local greasy spoon, with her 4 year-old daughter, Maya. You were relieved to hear from her, but not thrilled to talk about Geoff. Or even listen about Geoff. Or even have to acknowledge that Geoff was a halfway decent guy.

Something about him rubbed you the wrong way. He threw you 'that' look when you all went to the Hard Rock Café last month. It was that 'I'm-here-with-her-but-I'd-leave-with-you' look. Guys who give that look are like the guy you dated shortly after breaking up with your ex-husband - a "transition" guy - good for fun and nothing more.

"Tell you what," you said to Alisha, thinking on your feet. "Why don't you tell me about your date over breakfast? My treat. Old Yella won't start and I have somewhere to be at around one. Can you spare a ride for your girl?"

Alisha, always the concerned friend, started asking you a series of diagnostic questions based on her own experience with cars, which was painfully limited. You were already irritated this morning and listening to her tips didn't help your mood.

You wanted to shout, "Does it really matter what kind of squealing noise it made on Tuesday? It's not working today!"

But you didn't. You maintained your graciousness.

"Yes, yes. I tried all that, hon. Thanks. I'll worry about it later. How about you just swing by and pick me up? Then you can drop me off at the Doubletree on Ripley Road at this presentation I have to do."

Alisha agreed to the breakfast for ride exchange and arrived at your house within 15 minutes.

Minutes after gorging on a gyro omelet with fried onions and tomatoes, home fries, and a short stack of blueberry pancakes, you arrived at the hotel. You hugged your friend and leapt from the car like a gazelle, completely forgetting the black folder that contained your notes.

My Now…

…The same notes that you put off writing until last night. The notes that you NEED to do this speech because it's totally out of your realm. A little too personal. A little too real.

Anxiety strangles you when you look back out of the large hotel window and realize that Alisha's beige Toyota Corolla is no longer outside.

What are you going to do without those notes?

In the hotel corridor, a brick red scarf attached to a small, Latino woman catches your eye.

It is the same color red as your son's birthstone. Garnet.

After seeing that brilliant stone for the first time - eleven months post-separation - you visited the custom jewelry store across town and ceremoniously had the center diamond of your wedding ring replaced with a garnet. It represented the one good thing that came out of your failed marriage and marked the end of an era. You thought you would wear the ring on your right hand, yet it currently dwells among ordinary rings in a drawer, never seeing the light of day again.

"Alisha, where are you? Call meeeee," you whimper.

You look at your phone. No notifications.

22 minutes and you're on.

...for the Single Parent

"Excuse me, Miss." The garnet scarf-wearer stands peering up at you from eight inches below. Her jet black, wavy hair grazes her cheekbones meeting her grin from ear to ear.

"Yes?" you fake a smile.

"Is this the way to the Women in Business Empowerment Expo?"

"Yes, it's down the hall," you say as you nod to the left.

"Okay, gracias!"

You watch her glide down the hall in the direction of where you're supposed to be in approximately 20 minutes. You wonder if she is a "Woman in Business" and what she is expecting to get out of this program. You hope she's not expecting much from your keynote.

Seriously, a 5-10 minute keynote?

As you pace, your fingers ride the peaks and valleys of the bold, navy and cream paisley printed fabric that covers the walls.

"I need that folder," you say to yourself. "Why did I even agree to do this speech? Fifty bucks and lunch? My car is gonna cost at least two hundred dollars. Maybe I can trade a mechanic a website for it."

This is not the time to think about your car! Prioritize. You have to remember that speech.

"Why didn't I memorize it?" you ask aloud to no one in particular.

Memories of the last week dance around your mind. It feels like a blur of activity yet you strain to remember what you actually accomplished.

Checking emails.

Copy writing for a product you plan to promote on your blog.

Being a mom to little James.

Meetings with new clients.

Clearing up billing issues.

Part-time work at the Interior Design firm.

Laundry, dishes, dinners, lunches, volunteering at the kid's school.

Not forgetting to call your mother.

And of course, listening to the squealing sounds of Old Yella on every commute, hoping that your baby wouldn't crap out for good due to the cold temps. You always said you would "ride it 'til the wheels fall off", but you didn't imagine that as an actual reality.

Could the wheels really fall off?

Perish the thought.

You've worn so many hats since that woman reached out to you two weeks ago and asked you to speak at this event. You didn't have time to properly prepare. Now here you are with a busted vehicle, an MIA friend, and no notes.

…And you're supposed to be a spokesperson for 'Women in Business'?

Tsk. Tsk. Tsk.

You try to cut yourself some slack. You did the best you could. Or did you?

You check your phone again. 18 minutes until show time.

This is ridiculous. You're never this nervous before a speech. For almost five years, you marched undauntedly into high school classrooms in the toughest neighborhoods in the city. You gave presentations that had students howling with laughter while learning real-world skills to prepare them for life after graduation. As a guest speaker, you could quickly make a connection, rally the crowd and have them eating from your palms by the end of the class period. You took those experiences and expanded them into your own Corporate Training business, with the same outstanding results.

Yet, for this...you're nervous.

Why?

You swipe your phone to get to the call log, press "Alisha", and wait impatiently.

Voicemail.

She's probably on the phone with Geoff.

A few yards away, a gaggle of giggling women draw your attention. One is wearing a bright fuchsia sweater, so tight it looks like part of her skeleton. She is definitely the ring leader.

"Tiffany!" she squeals, noticing you. Freshly whitened teeth parade through the hall as this obviously put-together woman focuses in your direction. "I recognize you from your LinkedIn picture! I'm Cassie Murphy. Thanks for speaking here today! How are you?"

Her palms cup your extended hand.

"Hi, Cassie. Thanks for having me!"

She grabs your elbow like a nursing home aide, attempting to lead you to the room. "Let me show you to our room. We're right this way," she says.

"Oh, thanks," you say unshackling your arm from her friendly death grip. "But I'm waiting for someone."

Cassie stops in her tracks, eyes widened.

"...Another woman in business?" She asks, probing to find out if you shared those free tickets that were attached to her email. Too bad your printer has been broken for a month and you've gotten overly friendly with the print desk clerk at OfficeMax.

"Actually, I left my notes for this in a friend's car. We had breakfast this morning. I'm waiting for her to come back and bring them to me," you say.

A look of concern sweeps over Cassie's face. "You poor thing! Okay, well, let me get you a cup of coffee while you wait."

"Thanks so much, Cassie. That would be wonderful."

"How do you take it, hon?" She asks, in the tone of a Denny's waitress.

"A little cream and sugar, please."

She twirls around and skips down the hall to fetch your coffee at the ivory linen-wrapped refreshment table. Someone taps her on the shoulder and she turns around and hugs them.

"Good," you think, nervously peering out of the hotel window for Alisha. "A moment of peace."

Then, as it always does, your mind begins serving up thoughts with the fury of a Vegas slot machine.

"You should have prepared better," comes a voice from deep inside you.

Um, prepared? WHEN? I'm a busy woman.

Kinda.

I mean, I'm busy sometimes and I like to relax sometimes.

Should I feel guilty about needing a bit of me time? Moments of leisure? I TAKE CARE OF A HOUSE. AND RUN A BUSINESS. AND WORK PART TIME. AND CO-PARENT A GREAT KID. AND VOLUNTEER.

The voice in your head presses, "But really, bullet points and quotes? Come ooooonnn."

The internal dialogue pierces you like a hundred arrows. The truth hurts.

You strain to think back to the root of your procrastination.

It stemmed from the fact that you were repulsed by the title that Cassie gave you to work with: "Thoughts about being a single mother in business."

Single mother?

Do you really want to tell them what you think about 'single mothers'? You don't like being called that. That's for darn sure.

You look down the hall. Cassie is still talking with the woman, but she's obviously trying to end the conversation by stepping back and glancing in your direction.

"What's the problem with being called a 'single mother'?" The voice persists.

You cringe when you hear the term 'single mom' in the media. It sounds like they're begging for your pity before you hear their story. You don't consider yourself a 'single mother'. You are a mother who got divorced. But first and foremost, you are a human being; and you are not sure why you, as a human being, would need to tell someone about your relationship status within the first conversation!

Breathe, girl. Stop! Don't go crazy over semantics. Pull yourself together.

"Ugh. I need those notes," you mutter to yourself. "What time is it?"

Oh my gosh. 17 minutes.

You wonder what stopped you from just saying "no, thank you" to the woman's email request. You're a master at being assertive now. Your boundaries look like barbed-wire fences.

Your thoughts drift back to two years post-divorce. Walking through a foot of snow in your driveway, you carried both your laptop case and your 5 year-old to safety as the scary realization hit you; you would be the one to shovel the snow.

"So this is what a single mother feels like," you said to yourself.

In the puffs of pure white, you could see 12-inch holes leading to your door.

"Someone has been here today!" you breathed, barely audibly.

At that moment your son began chattering in your ear. "Me and Daddy came here today and got my game."

His words hit you like waves crashing on the shore.

"WHAT?!"

How many times have I told that man NOT to come to my house when I'm not here?

Yes, I get that it was once his house, too. But now he has a house...a house owned free and clear by his family, I might add...which enables him to skip writing a rent check each month. The key that I LET him keep was for emergencies. Not for him to go in and out as he pleases while I'm at work. Ever heard of privacy?

Your attention shifted back to little James.

"Well, it is up to you to remember everything you need for school and Daddy's house before you go. Your dad should not have to go out of his way, making special trips because of your forgetfulness. Before you go to bed tonight, you and I will come up with some solutions about how to avoid this in the future. Got it?"

Reaching your boiling point while fighting off the cold, Cleveland wind, you managed a smile at your son.

"I understand, Mommy." James replied. "You want me to be more responsible." The "s" in the word "responsible" slithered from his lips like the tongue of a hungry snake.

"Yes, James. I would like for you to be responsible and you will only learn how if you experience the natural consequences of your actions. That means no last-minute runs between houses when you forget something."

The two of you walked over the threshold into the house and James ripped off his boots, book bag and jacket. "Yes, I know. Daddy said the same thing to me."

Well at least we're on the same page about that! You thought. But I still don't like him in my home without me here. Time to sharpen those boundaries.

A tap on your shoulder jars you back to the present.

It's Cassie and one of her groupies.

"Tiffaneeeee," she sings as she hands you a steaming, pink and black mug etched in silver with the Women in Business Empowerment Expo logo. "We're starting in 15 minutes. Let me show you to the room and Charlene will stand here and wait for your friend. What was her name again?"

"Alisha," you cough, inhaling the strong coffee.

"Right…Alisha. Charlene, will you show Alisha to the room when she arrives?"

"Yes, woman, I will." Charlene chirps.

...for the Single Parent

Cassie leads you down the hall while going on about the nasty weather and your shared connections on LinkedIn. You zone out a bit while sipping your java.

As you enter the private conference room, Cassie takes your coat and ushers you to the presenter area. A bouquet of perfume tickles your nose as you walk through the huddles of women. A 20-something woman stops Cassie to ask a question.

Scanning the room, you recognize a few ladies from other events and wave at them.

And then you see Tina Goforth.

Tina's company, Rising Star Tutoring, LLC, is run exclusively by women. Tina knew your ex, intimately (you later found out). She was a casualty of his post-separation fling stage. Before she was narcissistic fodder for him, she was little James' second grade teacher...the one who played Homework God. The one who made that year harder than it had to be.

You flashback to when little James turned seven. Homework reared its ugly head in your home. Not the worksheets you did as a kid, consisting of 10 rows of 10 math problems or the memorization of weekly spelling words. No. This was hardcore homework...the kind that requires a mother to help her child locate long-lost household items that only MacGyver would find useful.

My Now...

That night, James looked up at you as you opened the can of sweet potatoes in heavy syrup, racking your brain as to what vegetable could offset all the sugar you were passing off as dinner. You had planned to make a trip to the grocery store that evening, but instead you let Mr. Soon-to-be-new-client drone on about his Lake Tahoe family vacation way past 5:30. Speeding to the daycare by 6:00, you decided to put off grocery shopping. The consequence of that choice was having to piece together a meal consisting of Tyson chicken nuggets, sweet potatoes and Lord knows what else.

"Mom?"

"Yes, sweetie?" you asked, fiddling through the vegetable drawer and locating a few leftover broccoli florets.

"Do you know where a ruler is?"

"A ruler?" stopped in your tracks, you looked at him incredulously.

"Yes. A ruler or a straight-edge. And a glue stick."

"Let me see that," you said, snatching the overly-Xeroxed worksheet after wiping your hands on your favorite plaid Ann Taylor skirt.

Skimming the directions, your eyes fell to the "What You Will Need" section of the page.

...for the Single Parent

A ruler or straight-edge

A glue stick

A piece of newspaper

Crayons or colored pencils

An adult

You read the last line again, growing red with rage.

Seriously? An adult?

How dare they plan my evening for me! Don't they know that I have things to do tonight? Important things. Things that will take place as soon as I get this dinner on the table!

The kid does his homework while I cook. That's the deal we have. Who are you so-called educators to change the deals made in MY house?

I have to provide the food, lights, heat, transportation, and now some teacher is giving ME homework? They want me to get involved more than looking over the page and initialing that planner every night? This is not the free babysitting I signed up for! I should go to a school board meeting.

My Now...

You were almost ready for an outburst when the lessons you taught at that "Managing Employee Emotions under Pressure" training class flooded your mind.

Girl, chill out. E-M-P-A-T-H-Y. You couldn't, for the life of you, remember what the empathy acronym stood for, but at least the pause helped soothe your mind.

These schools have no idea the pressure that you're under to simply get the child there on time, clean, fed and donning good manners. They have no idea how hard you work during the day or how you balance it all. And they definitely don't know the wisdom you try to impart to your son in that small window of time that you have him each evening.

You took a breath, and decided to let the idiotic school win the battle that evening.

"Alright, James, I'll get this stuff in a minute," you said.

You wondered what happens at your ex's house when the kid needs a ruler for homework. Let James tell it, Daddy has an abundance of every supply that could ever be necessary for homework and art projects. Drawers overflowing with sharpened pencils, new Crayola crayons and markers (not Dollar Store knock-offs like you have), watercolor paints, stickers for scrapbooking, and more... it's a veritable cornucopia of craftiness!

...for the Single Parent

After finding all of the items and placing them in front of your son, he looked up at you with your grandfather's smile.

"Thanks, Mommy. Me and Daddy couldn't find a ruler anywhere when I brought this home yesterday. You are the best Mom ever."

"And you're the best kid ever," you said as you tousled his curls, secretly cursing his teacher, Ms. Tina Goforth.

And here she is today, in all of her educational glory, promoting her new little project at the Women in Business Empowerment Expo. Tina Goforth along with her sidekick, Deb Fielding. You do not want to speak in front of either of them today. Especially not as unprepared as you are. Great.

Cassie bumps your shoulder while motioning to a chair where your coat drapes the back like a cape.

"Here you are, Tiff. Can I call you 'Tiff'?" she bumbles.

"Uh, sure," you say as you check your phone. No texts. No missed calls. 12 minutes to go. "My friends call me Tiff."

You keep your eyes on Cassie while gently placing your camel-colored hobo bag on the chair.

Cassie flashes you a grin. "Soooooo, Tiff. What are you going to share with our women today? I can't wait to hear your speech."

"Words of encouragement, I guess you could say. Some ideas that could help them along the way. It's a rough road being a woman in business."

Cassie nods and crouches down a bit, like she's helping a child learn to ride a bike without training wheels. Her voice softens as she says, "Many of the women here are single mothers."

There goes that term again, you think.

Cassie keeps going. "In speaking with them, we've found that many are overwhelmed with their various roles. Mother, business owner, woman, career-changer, divorcee, head of household... It's quite a quandary for this sub-section of the population. One thing we've noticed through surveys and workshops is that these women struggle to be authentic."

"Authentic?" You question.

"Yes. They say that they don't know who they really are, and they feel like they're wearing masks both in business and life in general. Do you happen to mention authenticity in your speech?"

"I could," you say, your smile matching hers. "Really hoping Alisha gets here soon."

You share a laugh and she begins to excuse herself. You stop her before she goes.

"Cassie, where is the restroom?"

"Right outside of that door, to the left."

You grab your purse and hurriedly brush past the Mary Kay booth and around the sign-in table decorated with pink roses.

You take a peek at your phone. Nine minutes.

Oh. My. Gosh.

Safely tucked inside the restroom, you approach the row of sinks, head to the third one, and peer into the mirror.

"Well, at least you have cute hair today," you sigh.

You continue staring in the mirror when the stall door opens behind you and a woman wearing an emerald green dress comes out. She spends a total of 2.6 seconds at the sink before ripping off a paper towel, tossing it in the trash and speeding out of the restroom.

You lower your body and sneak a peek under the stalls.

My Now...

You are alone.

You get up and look in the mirror again.

"Tiff, what are you going to talk about?" you ask your reflection.

You close your eyes and look up to the ceiling as the words pour out of you.

"I am a woman in business, just like most of you. Today we're going to talk about how being a mother affects your entrepreneurial decisions.

I'd like to start by saying that my son was deeply wanted. I knew that I wanted to be a mother and that his dad would be a great father. I thought that I could offer a lot to a child and I was willing to do the tough personal work necessary to be a good mother. I read a lot of parenting books, joined an online mother's group, and at age 25 after 3 years of marriage, we welcomed little James into the world.

Armed with years of experience babysitting and working with youth in schools, I thought I was prepared. In all my planning, I must have missed one small detail; children start off as babies, and I don't like babies.

The struggle was real, ladies. I battled myself daily. And in it, I realized that the books I had read and the moms online couldn't help me in the trenches. I had to do it my way.

Around his second year of life, an urge as strong as my biological need to mother emerged.

It was the call of business ownership. How many of you have felt that call?"

The mirror in the cold, grey public restroom doesn't respond.

"I started my first business at the age of nine, selling puffy-painted shirts to neighborhood kids and people at my church. I eagerly told everyone about my art and encouraged them to buy shirts while shoving neon-colored flyers in their faces. Entrepreneurship is in my blood.

Fast forward two decades. After working in corporate America for far too long, I became withdrawn and disillusioned. Between motherhood, untangling from my soon-to-be-ex spouse and my days spent in cubicle-land, I could hardly breathe without hyperventilating. I decided to quit my corporate job to start a business.

It was freeing to be the captain of my own ship for once and I remember that first year of being in business felt like an adventure. Absorbing information at night, while playing mother by day, I began walking into my dream…my vision…my goal for the future…something much bigger than simply building a business.

Some would say that there is no way that you can have a thriving business and be a good mother at the same time. Years ago, I would have agreed with them.

Now, with what I know, I see that one influences the other."

Tears well up in the corners of your eyes as you catch a glimpse of yourself in the mirror.

"As a mother in business, you may not be as successful as you would like to, but you will be enriched in other ways…intangible ways."

Your thoughts drift to Old Yella, sitting comatose in your driveway.

"The choices that arise when balancing motherhood and business are all a part of your training. I have a 15 year-old car because I choose enriching experiences with my son over paying a $400 car payment each month. I can only work at night after he's asleep or very early in the morning because I choose to make him lunch and drive him to school each day. I don't take appointments with clients on Fridays because I choose to volunteer in my son's class. It's like building a house with Lego's instead of bricks. Slowly, but surely.

But guess what? Right now, these choices work for me. For us. They give us opportunities for growth.

And I know that one day, when I finally reach my goals, I will be able to look back and say, 'I didn't miss a thing.'

Your children can be a big burden or your biggest cheerleaders. They can encourage your dream, even during your darkest hours, when YOU don't even believe in it. They give you something to work hard for."

You're crying now. Not just a sprinkle of tears. Full-on ugly-face cry.

You continue: "Ladies, just know that if you're a mom and a business owner, you may not feel it on a day-to-day basis, but joy, fulfillment and satisfaction will embrace you when you look back over your life. Even though it's hard now, and sometimes you don't know who you really are, you will feel a happy sense of deep gratitude for all the things you value and have attained in this journey. Remember that smooth seas don't make great sailors."

You hear shuffling coming from your left as the restroom door opens. Women begin piling in.

My Now...

You duck down and dash over to the paper towel dispenser. Dabbing your eyes and sniffing inconspicuously, you glance into the mirror once more before checking your phone.

Six minutes!

Sidestepping the women who have interrupted your sanctuary, you exit the restroom. You head into the open door of the conference room and Cassie gives you a wave from 12 feet away. She points to the stage and holds her hand up as if palming a basketball to let you know that you're on in five minutes.

Within moments, Charlene, the woman who was supposed to be waiting for your friend, is now standing center stage. Her short, natural afro is honey blonde, like the mane of a lion. Voices in the audience hush as they realize that it's time to start.

Charlene greets the crowd with a melodic roar. "Welcome back, ladies. I have the pleasure of introducing your keynote speaker for today."

As she reads the 500-word bio that you emailed to Cassie, you feel a tap on your shoulder. Alisha is standing there with her hand on her hip, her daughter, Maya, in tow.

"Girl, you made me come all the way back for this? I looked. It's like six bullet points. Be serious. You know you could have improvised and been fine."

With a lump in your throat, you take the black folder, and pull your friend in close for a hug. "Thanks, girl. I love you."

"I love you, too, woman." She grabs Maya's hand. "Oh, and I talked to Geoff about your car. His brother is a mechanic. He said he can go over and take a look at it today."

Surprised, you think that maybe that Geoff guy might have a redeeming quality. Maybe you'll give him another chance to impress you.

You smooth your hair, stand up straight, saunter onto the stage and look out into the sea of women greeting you with applause. Placing your folder on the podium, you pull out your notes and take in the scene. With a deliberate motion, you slide the notes back in, close the folder and breathe deeply.

"Good morning, ladies. Thanks for having me. I have some notes here, but I'm thinking that it might be better to speak from the heart today. Is that cool with you?"

A second wave of applause erupts in the room. A few women in the back make hooting sounds.

"Good. Because as both a mother and a business person, I can honestly say that since you'll never be totally prepared, you might as well be totally authentic."

My Now...

Michelda Johnson

Founder of Innovative Consulting, JEM Enterprises, Inc, d/b/a Edible Arrangements, and WaterWalker Ministries, Michelda Johnson has over 20 years of practical business experience and a breadth of knowledge as a tactical producer and strategic planner. Having managed human resource; training; project management; and financial functions in a myriad manufacturing, engineering/technical, distribution companies and churches, she provides practical, yet innovative solutions as well as strong leadership and program management. Michelda has senior leadership and management experience having been promoted to executive level positions at the early age of 25, and holds Bachelor of Science degrees in Management and Nursing.

WaterWalker Ministries provides Michelda with the opportunity to embrace a lifelong passion of motivating, encouraging, and PUSHING persons forward into their destiny and purpose. The entrepreneurial conferences are designed to stir up dreamers and then to provide them with tactical plans to successfully pursue within the foundational principle of God's plan first!

Twitter: @MicheldaJ
Instagram: micheldaj
Facebook: Facebook.com/waterwalkerministries

...for the Single Parent

But My God...
Michelda Johnson

Defining moments! Each of us has at least one moment in the course of our lives that reveals our own hidden ability, hidden struggle, hidden insecurity, and hidden strength. It is in those moments that we discover the essence of who we are. If you've had a defining moment, you remember it with clarity, almost down to the point of what color of shoes you had on when the other shoe dropped. In hindsight, you realize that defining moments produce a level of character and growth within you that you didn't believe was possible. The moment explores the inner qualities of your humanistic nature, and forces you to come face to face with all that you see in the mirror -- your good, your bad, and your ugly. If you allow it, your defining moment will produce beauty in ashes, and gorgeous pots from dirty clay.

One dictionary referred to defining moment as, "a point at which the essential nature or character of a person, group, etc., is revealed or identified". In other words, in that moment, who I truly am becomes visible. The key is to recognize that moment and allow the Holy Spirit to make the necessary adjustments. But My God is about recognizing that in our own strength we are useless against the frustrations of life but strong when we stand tall in His courage and strength. But My God refers to the scripture that is familiar to many… "But my God shall supply all of my needs according to His riches in glory by Christ Jesus"! (Philippians 4:19) But My God cancels out all of my own insecurity, my own fear, and my own inability to make things right. My biggest lesson learned through my NOW as a single parent was "but my God". I learned to trust, lean and depend on the shoulders of my Daddy - God!

My defining moment was the same event -- at two different times. See, I married and divorced, the same guy—twice. And although the circumstances differed, the result remained the same.

As an only child, and the product of a single parent household, I SWORE I would never divorce, nor would I raise my kids alone. I swore that I would live in the house with the white picket fence, a husband, 2.5 kids, a dog, stray cat, and a Volvo. That was my dream. However, life's circumstances made that dream a different reality.

My NOW as a single parent became a defining moment in my character… and, ultimately, in my walk with Christ.

There are several lessons that I learned that I hope will provide inspiration, encouragement, and focus to the parent that is discovering their NOW situation as that of a single parent.

...for the Single Parent

Forgiveness is such a powerful word when we walk in the power that the action provides. But true forgiveness is a hard task. It's difficult to imagine turning the other cheek when we are wronged; it's hard to smile SINCERELY as we pull knives from our backs. But because of the amazing love of Christ within us, and his limitless forgiveness of us, it gives us the strength and hope to forgive others.

At the root of unforgiveness is anger. Anger at being in this situation, anger at the actions of the other parent, anger and sometimes guilt—directed toward yourself for making certain decisions. Angry people are difficult to live with because that level of anger spills over into their everyday lives. Suddenly they are yelling at the kids, uptight and upset for no apparent reason. Anger will grow and fester and, if not checked, can easily become a root of bitterness. When we fail to remember the awesome promises of God, it's easy to feel despair, hurt, and pain when faced with a situation that isn't ideal.

Now, this may not be an issue for you as a single parent, but I know so many children that pay the price for the sins of their parents. So many beautiful babies become entangled in adult issues that they truly should not be concerned with. And, typically, it's a lack of forgiveness from the adults that drive situations further than what's necessary. If you are a blood-bought believer, then forgiveness is one of the foundational principles of our Christian walk. We have to choose the harder right over the easier wrong.

To truly be effective as a single parent, I must be able to forgive the other parent. I don't have to like them but I must forgive them. We've heard this all before, but as a reminder, forgiveness is not for them -- it frees you! Forgiveness will free you to a life of joy and happiness. Joy is not based on external situations but on an internal freedom that realizes that whatever is going on around me; my God is in control. When you walk in forgiveness, the joy of the Lord bubbles up on the inside of you. Forgiveness doesn't mean you become a doormat; but you can confidently walk in the character of Christ. A part of forgiveness is realizing that as God has forgiven me, then it is imperative that I forgive others. The freedom of forgiveness changes your platform to one of peace, it changes your attitude to one of contentment, and it soothes the aches and drives away the bitterness. Unfortunately many single parents struggle with a root of bitterness because of intense disappointment and the let-down in the expectations of the other parent. If not careful, that root of bitterness will affect you in so many other negative ways. Therefore, it's so much better for you physically, mentally, and emotionally to be at peace. Forgiveness will free you to be a better person, and a better parent for your children.

And so with forgiveness you receive this amazing view of love and the fruit it produces. So many parents look at their

...for the Single Parent

children through a tainted lens because it's based on the parent that they may look like, or act like. So when they see characteristics in the child that resembles the other parent, because of their own unforgiveness they begin to interact and react in a negative manner toward their child. Receiving God's love cleans the lens, and clarifies your sight. It solidifies your foundation and produces the fruit necessary to be amazing in your role of parent!

The next lesson that rapidly became evident was that "it wasn't about me"! As the mother of two (2) daughters at different stages of growth and development, I quickly had to learn to put aside my own feelings of grief (yes, divorce feels like grief), and focus on their needs. So in the moments when I wanted to cry like a baby, I had to smile, wipe a dirty nose, help with homework, and be the happy cheer-mom as I drove around typically 10-15 girls for practice and games.

As a single mother in my early 30's it would have been awesome to hang out with the "girls", go out on dates, etc., but my time was focused on raising my children to be contributing citizens to society and I took that responsibility seriously. The words of the scripture "deny yourself" suddenly leaped off the page and became real. My NOW as a single parent meant denying myself some of the pleasures that my other single friends were enjoying, and spending time watching Barney, and playing Chutes and Ladders.

My Now...

I don't mean to paint a dreary picture, I thoroughly enjoyed being a single parent. Because I'm not a huge birthday or Christmas present buying person, each year the girls selected a vacation spot for a 2-week vacation. The requirement was that it had to have historical significance, and we would do more than lounge by the pool. Those family moments of travel were awesome and served to broaden their horizon about other cultures. When the girls (who are now 19 & 21) get together, there are all kinds of funny stories and *"Do you remember when?"* moments. We can go for days talking about the fun things we did. At the end of the day, I never wanted them to feel like they were in a one parent household. I wanted them to feel blessed and loved. That also meant that I never stopped or impended their time with their dad......whether or not he paid child support! Again, it wasn't about me! In order for them to be stable and secure, I was willing to sacrifice whatever was necessary. I encouraged and purchased Father's Day gifts, Christmas presents, and extra family time with the other side of the family. Yes, they were my seed, but they were his as well. Don't allow your personal frustrations to spill over into frustrations for your children. People laugh at me today because I feel comfortable calling and communicating with my ex-husbands spouse. Well why not? We are all adults and the past needs to stay where it is -- in the past. My NOW to you is to "GET OVER IT" and start moving forward in your own purpose, focused on your beautiful children, and establishing a legacy for them that will last for generations. But My God means that He will provide the provision for YOUR vision of being an excellent parent. He will ensure that all of your needs are met, and that through whatever sacrifice you have to make; He will ensure that you receive a harvest and reap the reward. My motto was "short-term sacrifice for long-term gain"! Do the work and reap the benefits.

The time traveled quickly and I made our time as special as I could. However, the sacrifice is real. The key here is to remember that through every phase, God has equipped you with the tools to endure and to endure successfully.

Finally, be a PARENT! My role has and will always be that of a parent. If the side benefit of being a parent means you gain a friend, and your children an amazing respect for you then great! If being a parent means you have to make tough decisions, and sometimes be in the role of the "hammer", and they don't like you very much; then chose to be a parent. It is this role that doesn't feel particularly comfortable or warm and fuzzy but this role will certainly pay off in dividends. "Train up a child in the way he should go: and when he is old, he will not depart from it." Proverbs 22:6. Be a parent when it's cool and fun; and be the parent when it's hard, and tough, and when you KNOW they are rolling their eyes behind your back.

I have walked in many roles in my life, Vice-President, Board Chair, Director, Entrepreneur, Diva (LOL), Minister,

My Now...

Friend, Sister, Wife, and so many more; but the most amazing and fulfilling role I've ever had was that of a parent.

But My God.....He supplies all that you need to be the successful you in this challenging, vibrant, multi-dimensional, never a bored moment role of parent! Enjoy.....your NOW as a Single Parent!

...for the Single Parent

Part 2: Back on Track

My Now...

Isha Cogborn

Isha Cogborn is a life and business coach, speaker and trainer who helps people close the gap between their career and their calling. She's the president and founder of Epiphany Institute and author of the book, **5 Rules to Win Being You.** Her perspectives have been featured by media outlets across the country and beyond, including Cosmopolitan and Ebony magazines and ABC TV.

To find out how Isha can help you create the career of your dreams or to schedule her for your next event, Visit **CoachIsha.com**.

...for the Single Parent

Deferred, Not Denied: How to Get Your Dreams Back on Track
Isha Cogborn

"The test is positive. You're pregnant."

I saw her mouth moving, but I had a hard time comprehending the words coming out of the nurse's mouth at the campus medical clinic. I was only a week into my freshman year of college. My plan was to graduate, establish my career as a speaker and media personality, get married at 25 and have babies at 27 and 29. Instead, I was having my first (and only) child at 18 with no wedding ring in sight. After being voted "Most Likely to Succeed" in high school just a few months earlier, I was now labeled by statisticians as most likely to end up in poverty.

Parenthood is one of the greatest life changes you will ever experience. And whether you're doing it alone or with the support of a spouse, it can completely change the trajectory of your life. Our wants and needs take a backseat to our kids, and if you're like me, downsizing your professional ambitions seems like the responsible thing to do.

Instead of following the career path we're most drawn to, we often choose safer, more stable routes in the name of "what's best for the kids." We promise ourselves that when they're older or when we have more time, energy or money, we'll refocus on our original goals. But before we know it, we've traveled so far down the road that we can't even see our dreams in the rearview mirror.

If you became a parent early in life, you may not have even had a chance to truly figure out who you wanted to be when you grew up. And one day, you woke up to an empty nest trying to figure out what to do with yourself.

It's easy to feel like the window of opportunity to live your dreams is closed. But as long as you're still sucking air, you have a chance to become who you were created to be.

Closed Windows, Open Doors

I believe that we were all created to fulfill a purpose. At different points in our lives, we're presented with callings – specific opportunities to carry out our purpose. But not every calling is answered. Some opportunities may be missed due to unexpected life changes such as an unplanned pregnancy or the end of a marriage through divorce or death. Callings can also escape us because of paralysis brought on by fear or sheer laziness.

When we feel like we've missed our shot in life, we can put a lot of pressure on our children to run with the ball we dropped. It can also lead to unhealthy behaviors like:

- Overeating or drinking
- Indulgent spending
- Toxic relationships
- Excessive partying
- Negativity and despondency

A fancy car, lavish vacation or pint of Ben and Jerry's will only temporarily mask the void that can only be filled by your purpose. Don't fall prey to the lie that the only thing worthwhile you'll ever do is raise a child or that your best days are behind you. While the window of opportunity to fulfill a calling may close, your purpose itself never expires. You'll be presented with another shot at fulfilling your purpose, though it may look a little different this time around.

Wherever you are today, don't focus on the windows of opportunity that you feel are closed. Instead, look for new doors that are opening. What dream or goal did you put on hold because you became a single parent? Is it still important to you today? If so, you owe it to yourself, your children, and the people who will benefit from what you have to offer to pursue it.

New Seasons, New Approaches

Just like the world around you, you are constantly evolving. Have you ever thought about how much better equipped you are today to fulfill your purpose than you were before? Consider these factors:

More Knowledge and Experience – What do you know now that you didn't know before? What talents have you refined or new skills have you gained?

Expanded Network – Who have you connected with that can help to open new doors or equip you to walk through them? Are there people that you can partner with to increase your effectiveness?

Technological Advances – When I was pursuing a media career in the early 90's, local news was one of the only entrances to the field. Today, there are hundreds of cable channels and of course, YouTube. Small businesses are now able to compete with global enterprises because technology is leveling the playing field by lowering costs and allowing entrepreneurs to have a broader reach. The same goes for artists and entertainers. How can technology help you?

Wisdom and Maturity – There are some benefits to be gained from just being on the earth longer. Instead of looking at your age as a liability, how can you use it to your advantage?

Another benefit of wisdom and maturity is that the "why" behind your goals and dreams often become less self-centered. Don't be surprised if your professional aspirations change because of that. Evolving as a person isn't the same as giving up on your dreams. That's why there's more than one way to fulfill your purpose.

5 Tips to Reignite Your Dreams

You wouldn't lie to anyone and tell them that being a single parent is easy, would you? Just the same, I won't tell you that pursuing your dreams will be, either. But much like parenting, it's worth the effort.

Here are five actionable tips to help you bring your goals back to the forefront and make meaningful, measurable progress:

Write the Vision

Before you start constructing the roadmap, make sure you have a clear picture of where you want to go. What do you want to accomplish? How do you personally define success? Paint a mental picture of what your life looks like when you get there – then get it out of your head and put it on paper.

Once you have it written down, review your vision every day. By doing so, you'll be more conscious of doors of opportunity opening around you. If you're really serious, create a few positive confessions to speak out loud over yourself and your life aligned with where you want to go. You can even create a vision board.

Stay Engaged

As the saying goes, "Out of sight, out of mind." If you don't have people around you doing what you want to do, it's a lot easier to give up on it. No matter how busy you are or how few resources you have, there are ways to pursue your dreams. No excuses. Here are a few suggestions with varied degrees of effort. Pick one or two that could work for you or think of some on your own:

1. Read one article a week or one book a month that will help equip you to fulfill your vision. You can find a set time or day to read, or work it into the nooks and crannies of your schedule. Don't turn on the TV – read instead!
2. Join an organization that will help you gain knowledge or build a network that will contribute to your success. If your involvement in the group is a credibility booster to the outside world, consider volunteering for a committee or a leadership position.
3. Follow five industry leaders on social media and pay attention to what they're talking about. What publications or organizations do they reference? What trends are they talking about and how does that affect the work you'll be doing? Make meaningful comments on their posts and share them with your network as a sign of appreciation. It may even put you on their radar!

4. Volunteer to help someone who is doing what you want to do. Don't let the fact that you aren't getting paid serve as an excuse to give less than your best effort.
5. Schedule informational lunches, coffee dates or phone interviews with someone in your desired industry each month. Find out how they got where they are, what they would do differently if they were starting over today, what skills you'll want to focus on building and who else they suggest you talk to.

Build Your Personal Brand

A strong, authentic personal brand begins with knowing what problem you can confidently solve. If you're not confident in your ability, you'll be hesitant to "put yourself out there." How do you build confidence? Through the knowledge or experience you already possess or the results you have already achieved. And they don't have to be directly correlated to what you're looking to do next, either. How can you transfer the knowledge or lessons learned in previous experiences?

After you've identified the problem you can confidently solve, focus on how you can differentiate yourself from others who do what you do. We live in a noisy world. Expecting your work to speak for itself just isn't good enough – you have to make sure the right people are listening! Look for ways to begin positioning yourself with stakeholders. This could be sharing your work on social media, community involvement or activism, blogging or even writing a book. If you don't want to create your own content, consider curating high-quality information from others that the audience you want to connect with will enjoy. Here's the bottom line: You want people to associate you with the work you want to do, not just the work you're doing now or as your kid's mom or dad.

And finally, remember that everything you do either strengthens or diminishes your brand. This includes the quality of your work, your attitude, posts on social media, your personal appearance, and even your mobile ringtone! Do your best to ensure that everything you say and do reflects the way you want the world to see you.

Nurture Your Network

Networking is more than collecting business cards and LinkedIn connections. Doing it right means finding ways to be helpful to the people you're connected to. Make nurturing your network a deliberate activity by setting a goal to have a certain number of lunch or coffee dates or phone chats each month. The focus of these meetings shouldn't be what you want from them. Instead, find out what they're working on and how you can help them reach their goals. Just because someone is higher up on the food chain doesn't mean you don't have something valuable to offer. Your unique perspective could help them improve their work, or you may have someone else in your network that would be a great connection for them.

Don't fool yourself into thinking simply following influential people on Twitter will make a difference when it comes to fulfilling your dreams. Remember this: It's not who you know, it's who knows you.

Be Patient

You didn't expect your child to start school the week after they were born, did you? So why aren't you more patient with the process of achieving your dreams? A number of factors impact the rate of your success. There are factors you can control, such as increasing your levels of knowledge and experience. But there are also things you can't control, like the economy, adverse trends in your industry, et cetera, et cetera.

There will also be times when the effort you invest doesn't yield the results you anticipated. Will you throw in the towel when things don't go as planned? Imagine if you gave up on parenting because your kids didn't always do what you told them to. Life won't always do what you want it to, but that's not a reason to quit. Take time instead to evaluate your plan and ensure that you're working on the right things at the right time with the right approach.

No matter how or when you became a single parent, don't accept the delay of your dreams as the death of them. If you still have a purposeful vision inside of you, pursue it with the energy it deserves. I can't imagine how empty my life would be today if I hadn't gotten back on the road to pursuing my dreams. There have been plenty of potholes and detours along the way, but it's a worthwhile journey that has allowed me to help more people than I'll ever know.

One of the greatest examples we can set for our children is to follow our dreams. When we believe all things are possible in our lives and act accordingly, they'll believe it for themselves, too.

...for the Single Parent

My Now...

Nikia Brown-Sweeney

Nikia is the Executive Director of Building a Better Me Mentoring (BABM) and has been an advocate for youth for over a decade. "On a mission to succeed and destined to achieve" is a motto that has inspired Nikia to advocate for youth and women. Providing a platform for girls to believe that it's their unique traits and personality that makes them beautiful is the nucleus of the BABM program for youths. Nikia's recent addition to the program features outreach efforts to inspire women to take on a more active approach in the parenting of their children while teaching them how to create opportunities to explore and achieve their personal and secular goals. Serving in the role of Corporate Public Relations Director for two Maryland based companies has allowed Nikia to reach out to audiences and personally impact thousands of lives in the community with educational outreach programs designed to motivate individuals to make positive life changes. "The little lady with the big voice" enjoys motivating through public speaking at seminars, workshops, community events, and corporate events.

Office: (443) 360-0036
Email: Pinkgowns@gmail.com
www.TreasuredGems.org
www.MaryKay.com/NSweeney

...for the Single Parent

A Lesson from an Octopus
Nikia Brown-Sweeney

"I changed my name" reads the sign posted on my bedroom door. Its 6'oclock Wednesday morning, the alarm is going off and as I listen to the soothing sounds of nature (the alarm ringtone), I'm inspired to do something different. Once the alarm that wakens me to start my work day is silenced, my mental health day begins. The sign on the door lets the kids know that mom is off work, securely, and personally. My name has changed, and it's not "mom" today.

Another restless night, I've been in bed for eight hours, but slept for less than half. Tossing and turning with streaming images of all the things I have to do today, tomorrow, next week, and even by the end of the month. A picture of an octopus enters my memory as I contemplate my agenda for the day. The "to do" list, like the McDonald's menu, rarely ever changes. By now there is a systematic approach to getting things done; but why am I so tired?

Like most moms, the octopus perfectly depicts the struggle to maintain the many responsibilities that come along with parenting. This eight-armed creature has abilities in connection to parenthood worth examining. There are lessons to be learned from this self-sacrificing sea "mom." Her dedication to her offspring is remarkable. Her home, immaculate, by sea standards, is prepared so she can lay her eggs. For several weeks she stays with her eggs and takes on a defensive stand to protect them from harm. While she's caring for the needs of her soon be offspring, her basic needs are severely neglected. Shortly after the hatching of her offspring, she dies of starvation.

As intelligent humans with common sense, the thought of starving ourselves to death to care for our children might appear far-fetched; are we starving in other areas of our lives? Could we become so consumed in protecting our children from the scars of divorce, that our over compensation becomes a way of life that tires us out? The octopus's dedication to her offspring preserved them alive, but the weighty cost was her life. Offspring of octopuses are designed to maintain life without direction from their parents; however human children lives cannot sustain without parental guidance.

Parents, you are to be commended because if you are reading this book, you are an active part of your child's life. The following questions will be answered in this discussion to help you maintain or develop a healthier lifestyle that will lead to balance in your life? How can you find a balance in parenting while making time for yourself? What practical suggestions could help you examine your schedule to make time? How does my children benefit when I set an example in being balanced? Unfortunately, Divorce is a common battle today but divorce wars, doesn't have to have casualties. We can heal our children's wounds from divorce with love, patience, and balance.

Time...Your Most Valuable Asset

Twenty-four hours a day plus seven days a week equals one hundred and sixty eight hours a week. That's all we have and according to the Grand Creator of the Universe, that's all we need! Does our schedule revolve around our family and our personal needs or is it vice versa? We may not be able to add an extra hour to the day or a day to the week, but with careful planning we can make the most of our time. Look at the chart below and ask yourself, what areas of your life you can make adjustments to open up opportunities to use your time wisely.

Sample Weekly Schedule

Activity	Time used	Time Left
Work/Commute	50	118
Sleep (8 hours a night)	54	64
Family/Weekend *	26	38
Exercise 4 times a week	10	28
Add an Activity		
Add an Activity		

*Family time includes 8 hours on Saturday and Sunday with 2 hours each evening during the week.

In the sample schedule, the basics are covered: job, sleep, family activities, and exercise with a little more than a day left. What would you do with those 28 hours? Pick the start of a week and track your day to day activities. Get specific so that you can achieve results. Every hour counts especially if there are after school programs, sports, religious activities, and other weekly responsibilities.

Just Say No!

"Just do it" might work for Nike, but for you, sometimes you have to say no. Practice makes perfect and once you've mastered the art of discernment, balance suddenly appears. Some of us are super heroes eagerly looking for a phone booth to change our clothes so we can save our neighbors, relatives, employees, friends, and even the school's PTA. Don't get me wrong. I personally love helping people, it's rewarding and leaves me with a feeling of joy. But there are times when I put way too much on my plate and my family suffers. If you have found that everyone comes to you for help, consider it a compliment, but use wisdom in deciding if you really are capable of handling it. "No" doesn't have to mean never, it could mean not right now, or with a few modifications, you can make it happen.

...for the Single Parent

A Return on Your Investment

Time, unlike money, cannot be returned, but if it is well spent, it pays tremendous dividends. How are you depositing your time? Is it being eaten up by poor investments or at a standstill with no documented progress? The chart illustrated above, showed that it's possible to accomplish many tasks with time left over. Remember the mother octopus, tending for the needs of her children came first, but due to lack of attention to her needs caused her demise. Listed below, you'll find different aspects of life to evaluate.

JOB: In today's economy, it's a blessing to have a job. The state of the economy has placed a fear in many who have become workaholics in order to maintain employment. Are you a hard worker? Of course you are, but are you going overboard with your job duties? Can you find balance in your work schedule and responsibilities so that all your energies are not sapped by clock-out time?

CHILDREN: It may take money to shelter, clothe, and feed them, but quality time is priceless! Take a moment to think about a time during your childhood that meant the most to you. Those memories might not include a time where significant money was spent or a shopping spree for school clothes. One of my favorite childhood memories is the time I'd spend with my dad on Sunday evenings to pick up ice cream for the family. Another memory is the long drives I'd take with my mom so that we could just talk. When your children share their childhood experiences with their children, what memories will they hold dear. Parents with the joint custody arrangement can be faced with a challenge when it comes to quality time. To keep track of my schedule with my daughters, I use a highlighter in my planner, so that I plan around their time with me. Special dates and events are noted as far in advance as possible so that I don't miss them. Is your children's participation in sports, organizations, or clubs, becoming overwhelming? Ask for help! Share the transportation or other obligations associated with the activities with their other parent or responsible relative. Household work takes time and its fun when more hands are involved. Delegate, delegate, delegate! Create a personalized schedule with age appropriate chores around the house so they feel a sense of responsibility in their home. Besides, we're not raising kids, we're raising adults. Quality time includes preparing our little ladies and gentlemen for adulthood.

PERSONAL: Take a deep breathe then exhale. Do this five times with your eyes closed. No really, try it, it works! Did you feel it...the sense of calm from this relaxation technique? No longer scattered-brained and tired, you can end this chapter motived to take positive steps. Get out that tablet, I Pad, planner, journal book, spiral notebook, or take one of the twenty composition notebooks you brought from Wal-Mart at the start of the school year and get busy! Real goals are written with a plan to achieve them. Communicate your realistic goals to those that will hold you accountable. Never be afraid to delegate responsibilities, ask for help, or say no. As you calculate your time, make time for your health and well-being. Schedule your visits to the doctors as far in advance as they will allow. Get to know your body by not turning a blind eye to pains and discomfort. Physical fitness is excellent for the mind and body. Besides if we don't take care of ourselves, whose going to take care of the kids?

Although the earthquake named divorce may be final, the aftershocks are still at work. Regardless of the reasons for divorce, who filed first, who re-married first, there are wounds that take time to heal. All the research shows that divorce can have negative physical and emotional effects on everyone involved. Our children deserve a chance to be happy in a balanced stable environment. We set the example. A successful parent is a successful person first. Successful people prioritize, realize, and organize their lives with care. Carefully organize your schedule and goals so that you can give necessary attention to the needs of your children while caring for your own.

My Now…

Clara Morrison

Clara Morrison believes in living with a brave, unyielding passion. Clara writes and edits in both the creative and technical fields. Her published freelance works range from poetry and short stories to advertising and technical publications. An elementary teacher by profession, Clara earned dual Bachelor's degrees in graphic design and elementary education from The University of Alabama Huntsville. She's very excited about her most recent writing project, a song writing collaboration. In her spare time, Clara and her daughter own and operate *ShawnCezanne,* a handbag and fashion accessory company. At home, Clara enjoys being a "supermom" and spending time with her two children, Morgan and Sam, and her cat, Mirabella. After a day at school with little kids, Clara spends her "Me Time" at the gym or enjoys a little "retail therapy".

Contact Clara at claramorrison@rocketmail.com

...for the Single Parent

The Me Time Principle
Clara Morrison

From the time your newborn was born, you've been hopelessly in love with your child. Fabulous! Your world immediately changed and you became the fierce protector, sworn to provide absolutely everything within your power, no matter the sacrifice. Congratulations mom or dad, you are now the ideal, modern parent. You sacrifice your "Me Time" to get in the daily grind and still make all those play dates, special lessons, ballgames, and kiddie social events. So now what? You wake up one day a single parent, busting your ass to do what has been engrained in you from day one: being the selfless giver. How does a single parent take *Me Time* and still give their kids everything they need? Let's explore all the elements of that question.

The Giver

It's wonderful to give of yourself. Giving someone, especially a child, your time is a selfless gift. Being a giver is admirable and noble. Some of the most popular folks in history have been outstanding givers; however, you are neither Mother Teresa nor Jesus Christ. Practice self-sacrifice in moderation and do something nice for yourself. Sound selfish? Good. Sometimes, it's okay to be selfish. Your life is filled with the reality of balancing your time and energy between family, work, and whatever else you can squeeze in. Does the rest of what you are squeezing in contain regular time set aside just for you?

Just Like Mom

My mom is the blueprint for selfless giving. She always loved taking care of people - especially her family. After twenty-plus years of marriage and sacrifice she was suddenly a single parent ...and one bitter chick. So what did she do? (Besides hate on my dad at every turn because he left a spouse that gave her time to everyone except their marriage.) She kept on giving - overcompensating, outworking, and controlling everyone. Did she take care of herself and take the Me Time she needed? Never. Her idea of Me Time was locking the door while she was in the bathroom. Did she seize the opportunity of a new love interest when it came her way? Nope. She couldn't bear to put anyone before her [grown] kids and grandkids. Opportunity sadly missed. Did she ever do one thing that was completely self-motivated? Not that I remember. Now her health is failing, she's aging, and her grown kids struggle to meet her many, changing needs.

Flash forward several years. Suddenly, I am the divorced parent, drowning in my life's obligations. It's been all about my kids since I knew they existed. One day, something profound happened and, I heard an unmistakable voice within me say, "Hey! Remember me?"

...for the Single Parent

> *It was a vibrant, but lost, young woman with big dreams. She was buried under years of obligation and sacrifice. I looked in the mirror and reflected on whom I had become and thought, "Damn! No wonder I look and feel like hell. I never take time to take care of or connect with myself. I had become my mother—painted façade, others first, self last."*

My Message

You and your family deserve the very best "YOU" that you can be. However, in order to be that person, you have to make an effort to give yourself what you need. It's okay, in fact it is *essential*, to put yourself first...at least once a day. Trust me. When it comes to being an effective parent or anything else, you cannot let your personal needs get continuously pushed to the back burner. That pressure cooker will explode and you will be left with a huge mess to clean up. Let's explore how to prevent that and become a more effective parent by creating a healthy dose of selfishness in your daily life.

Me Time Overview

Who? If you're reading this enlightening, new book, then you are likely interested in a few pointers on how to better juggle being a single or divorced parent. Most of what you are reading in this book is how single and divorced parents successfully navigate life's daily issues alone. However, you may find much of this chapter is applicable to anyone, regardless of children or marital status. (I actually know a few married friends who need this advice as much as anyone else. So feel free to share this info with all of your friends.)

What? You are an important part of your children's lives and they need you to be on your "A" game as much as possible. You cannot be at your best without nurturing your *elemental self.* It's going to take a little selfishness on your part, to get there, but you and your family will certainly reap the benefits.

When? Taking time for you is a daily process. It's like saving money. Sometimes you can put back more than others but it's not saving if you just write yourself a check in emergencies. Like saving money, it takes planning and consistency to take your *Me Time.*

Where? The beauty of the "Me Time Principle" is that it is completely flexible - a fluid activity with interchangeable components that can actually fit your busy schedule. Let's unlock where you can apply this formula to your life.

Why? If you take care of yourself, then chances are you will feel better and perhaps be around longer to enjoy your good mental and physical health with your family and other special people in your life. At the very least you'll become a more pleasant person to tolerate. Blowing off steam and regrouping fulfills an elemental need. No one is going do it for you. You owe it to yourself and those you love. Get going and (to quote a popular *Nike* phrase) "Just Do It".

How? Half the battle here is self-allowance. The rest is split between reorganization of a few obligations and resources. Keep reading. We'll explore the entire formula.

Your Elemental Self

What are the elements that make up who you are? Of course there are the physical, mental, emotional, psychological, and spiritual parts of you. Are there more? Are you more than the sum of your parts? Of course you are. You are uniquely and wonderfully you! No one knows you like you do. Are you in touch with your elemental self? Which part of your elemental self would you like to improve or nurture more?

What are the elements of your *life*? They are different from the elements of *yourself*. Of course there are your children, your family, your career, your social circle, your finances, your daily obligations, your goals, and the rest of your baggage. The elements of our lives can often become quite daunting as well as very rewarding.

Often the elements of our lives overtake the elements of our elemental selves and we become disconnected and overwhelmed. Usually, we sacrifice the nurturing of our elemental selves to deal with the elements of our lives. For example, I have often been guilty of neglecting my physical needs because my job has me too stressed to take time to feel like planning and preparing a healthy meal then going for a brisk, stress-relieving walk. Instead I've opted for the fast-food drive-thru, chemical-filled, deep-fried crap-in-a-bag then dragging my tired ass home to crash into my recliner. Basically, I let the elements my life overtake the needs my elemental self.

Unfortunately, I've been guilty of dragging my kids into this loser lifestyle too. What have I taught them, other than don't disturb the witch when she takes to her recliner? That I don't value myself enough to take time to love and nurture my body, mind, and spirit. What a horrible example! Changing that is proving to be one of my greatest, yet most rewarding, challenges ever.

Discovering the Me Time Principle

I'll begin with an obvious disclaimer: *The Me Time Principle* does not promote child neglect or excuse anyone from being a responsible parent. The purpose of being selfish enough to take time for yourself is a suggestion to help you better deal with your day to day stress and be a more effective parent.

The Me Time Principle can only have as much impact and power as you give it. As you use it and begin to see the benefits, the momentum of nurturing your elemental self and regaining control of the elements of your life may surprise you. It can spill over into many aspects of your life. To say, "Try it. You'll like it," is a bit cliché but if the shoe fits….buy them both and run like hell in them. (You may quite literally be running for your life.)

Me Time is not a new discovery that I am marketing through this book. It is merely what I call the time I take for myself, on a regular basis, to do something to unwind and let go of my internalized, daily stress, to reconnect to my positive energy. It's not always easy. Many days, I'd just rather crawl into bed. Honestly, I occasionally do. No one is perfect. However, my *Me Time* not only helps me feel better, focus, and relax, it also helps me be a more effective parent [and teacher] because I'm less stressed and more patient. Many of you have heard the old saying, "If Mama ain't happy, then nobody's happy." This often applies to dads too. I cannot stress enough the importance of taking care of your mind, body, and spirit so you can bring home the you that your family deserves. The results are truly cumulative if you do….and unfortunately, cumulative if you don't, as well.

Fume Fatale

I have a co-worker that often says, "I hate that my students get the best of me and what's left over for my own kids is the rest of me."

Personally, I don't know how she does it. She's Wonder Woman and Super Mom wrapped up in a ball of energy. Widowed mother of triplets, one with special needs. Newborn just joined her brood. Her triplets are the same age as the students she teaches. This Wonder Chika never misses a kid event, team game, social event, family gathering, and (if that were not enough) she co-manages a successful home-based business on the side. She takes her daily drama in stride and everyone in her flock always arrives looking fab and fashion-forward. Some people are the exception in life. If this fierce Warrior Mom can accomplish this as well as she does without her Me Time, imagine what she could do if she had the regular time she needs to reconnect with her elemental self. She'd be even more of a force of nature than she is now. Not everyone is this strong. Though she humbly admits she doesn't take the Me Time she needs, sometimes I wonder if she runs on fumes.

Are you running on fumes? Do you take your *elemental self* for a brisk walk, quick jog, quiet mediation, or yoga class? Do you put your housework or paperwork aside to escape into a non-kid movie or age-appropriate book? Do you leave your work at work and hit the gym to relieve your stress before you walk through your door at night? Do you let go of an occasional parental obligation and let your ex or co-parent take the lead? Do you allow yourself an occasional night out with friends or someone special? If you're answering *no* to these questions, then keep reading. If you're not, read on anyway because you likely know someone who needs this advice.

Remember, you are *not* a superhuman! Your essential self does not run efficiently on fumes. The freeway of life has some tricky, navigational challenges. Refuel and reconnect for the ones you love and give them (and everything in our life) the best of you.

A Few Good Myths

Here are a few myths that we too often believe about being a good parent that could interfere with taking our Me Time.

Being a good parent means always putting your child's needs first.

Self-sacrifice is the name of the parenting game.

They grow up so fast. I've got to be there for them....for everything.

My kids deserve to have it better than I did when I was a kid.

Selflessness sets a good example for my kids in their future relationships and molds their future parenting skills.

I have to compensate for my lousy ex or co-parent.

My Now...

Debunking the Myths

BULLSHIT! All of it....plain and simple.

We live in a society that has confused self-sacrifice for the sake of our children with good parenting and helped propagate a mindset where we judge ourselves by how much time and material goods we give our kids. We try to be "both parents" at once and use over-indulgences to alleviate our guilt. We over-involve our kids in a deluge of activities and keep attendance tabs on our exes or co-parents then use it against them. We've become a generation of helicopter parents who enable co-dependent teens who drive us nuts when they rebel by thinking for themselves as they approach adulthood. We work and sacrifice so our children can have it "better than we did" and wonder why they cannot function without us bankrolling their young adult lives. Plain and simple, we've taken the loving act of parenting and turned ourselves into nagging, control freaks who have spawned an entitled generation of people expecting to be spoon-fed life. Then we wonder [later] why their relationships become dysfunctional when their mate doesn't live up to the fairy tale endings our little princesses and kings have in their heads. Of course I'm no guiltless saint in this matter but I've discovered a truth that is setting me free.

...for the Single Parent

What the Cluck?

The first year my middle school son was in the high school marching band, I never missed a beat. I followed that band bus and hung tough with the rest of the hovering hens. The schedule was grueling - and that was just for me. The next year, when my son was in the 8th grade, I made up my mind. He's a smart, responsible young man. He was well supervised and mature enough to handle it. Moreover, he knew to follow all the rules or he's out of band. I hated letting go but I put him on that band bus, every now and then, and said, "Call me when the bus gets back."

Why did I do such a "heartless act of abandonment"? Because when I was fourteen years old, my parents occasionally did the same thing for me. I remember loving the feeling of independence. I remember the poor girl who was my teammate, whose mother sat at every, single practice and every game. We all secretly called her "Mother Clucker" and felt sorry for her kids because she hovered like a neurotic hen. (I even recall a few chicken clucks some of us mean girls would cackle out when she fluttered by after her daughter.) Classic helicopter parent.

When my daughter moved off to college, my son told me I was a Chinook (double blades, big-ass hoverer, carries lots of baggage) and he hoped I wouldn't hover so when he moved out. I had to start with him somewhere, so 3 months later, the week between Christmas and New Years, I put that fourteen year old smartass on a band bus and sent him to perform at the Outback Bowl in Tampa, Florida, over 600 miles away.

It killed me, not being there with him. I was so proud that I cried as I watched those kids on TV. Although my son asked me not to go on his trip, he didn't have to say why. I already knew. It was his experience, not mine. I remembered my parents putting my fifteen year old butt on a bus going to my state track meet and lovingly saying, "Good luck, behave, good bye." (No cell phones back then and collect calls were for emergencies only.) But I loved it! Sure, I missed them...for 5 minutes...but I owned my experience.

By the time my younger brother came along and was doing these same activities, my parents were divorced and Mom was keeping tabs on which activities our father did and didn't attend. We were all there. My brother never had a minute's peace and never experienced anything alone - good or bad. In his eyes, we were all there to worship and serve "the chosen one." (He was also in his 40's before he and his wife and kids moved out of our mother's house. Enablers beware.) Your babies need Me Time to grow.

Yours, Mine, and Theirs

Remember the baby diaper commercial that used the slogan "Live and learn...and then get Luvs"? Babies are great! But we keep babies close and we manage their lives for them. When those sweet babies grow up and try to spread their wings a little, too often parents forget that those same babies need to stand on their own...and occasionally fall. It's hard to give up that control. What does this have to do with your *Me Time*? Older kids need their "Me Time" too. I'm not saying make them quit baseball or ballet so you can perfect your ass in the gym. I'm suggesting you sit your teen down and explain that they can occasionally do some things on their own, as long as they behave responsibly. Use it as a growing experience for you both.

Do you know someone who is a helicopter parent? How about someone who over-commits their time to their kids' extracurricular activities then makes flimsy excuses why they don't take time for themselves. I'm sure you won't be drummed out of the collective if you choose not to participate in absolutely everything *The Joneses* do. Just be sensible and practice moderation. Teaching your child to spread themselves too thin doesn't give them time to excel at one special thing - then no one thing is special. Furthermore, they don't get the *Me Time* they need [to just be a kid.] Use your head for something other than looking pretty. Think about it. Everyone needs *Me Time*. If you give them theirs then you are more likely to get yours too.

My Me Time is Not Your Free Time

We've pretty much established that you need to take time for yourself on a regular basis. Remember, no one is going to do that for you. It's very unlikely your kids will one day come to you and say, "Mom (or Dad), you need to take a break from attending to my needs so much and get out and do something nice for yourself." If they do, beware - especially if they're over 13. You may come home early one night and discover there's an impromptu house party at your crib.

A footnote on your *Me Time*: mix it up now and then. Change your activity; vary your times, if you can. Varying your schedule keeps you from falling into a boring rut and it keeps your older kids on their toes. Never, ever let your teens confuse your *Me Time* with their *free time*. They *may* turn it on you and you *could* end up working to stay ahead of them. Trust me. Even the good kids sometimes plot behind their parents' backs. (I did and I'm sure you did too.) Don't let that scare you off though. Set and enforce ground rules and consequences with all your children about your *Me Time*.

Dragging Others into Your Self-Sacrifice

We often sabotage our *Me Time* by dragging others into our network of givers and takers. It's often hard to know where to draw the line, especially where children and family members are concerned.

Many years ago, when my daughter was born, she had some serious health issues that required a lot of special attention. Being a new mom, the self-sacrificing parenting skills I learned from my own mother naturally kicked in. My life became all about my daughter's wellbeing. To say it consumed me is a colossal understatement. I was transformed into a shadow of my former self. My mother praised me as the best mother

...for the Single Parent

she knew. I ate her praises up and rarely allowed anyone to help me with my daughter, for fear that no one could do for her as I could.

Within a few years of marrying me, my hubby defaulted into my parental obligations and our giving natures drew many extended family solicitations for help ...and unfortunately the drama that entailed. Our lives were so wrapped up in other people's responsibilities, we couldn't move forward in our own relationship. Our lives left no time for us. Our relationship became about everything else but our marriage. We became stagnate. Like putrid water, we were poisonous to each other.

What's Love Got to Do With It?

Why is dragging others into your self-sacrifice so unhealthy and how is this relevant to being selfish enough to take your essential *Me Time*? No one wants to be used. While very few people will agree that young children consciously use their parents, many people know of *adult* children who shamelessly put their responsibilities upon other family members, especially parents. Do you think these people just woke up one day and decided, "Hey, I think I'm going to take advantage of my family for my own personal gain?" Not likely. More often than not, a well-meaning relative enabled them at a very young age.

While sacrificing your time for family, friends, and causes is noble, please do it with caution. You could easily lose a lot of yourself, your valuable time, and quite possibly your money. You could be setting yourself up in a co-dependent relationship with someone you love, to whom it's hard to say no, while impairing their independence. Furthermore, drawing your loved ones into the dramas associated with your unhealthy, co-dependent relationships will likely create resentment. You may also be teaching your own children, by example, that love equals giving, in fact sacrificing, parts of themselves they are not comfortable giving up. Instead, I now tell my own children to never sacrifice their own values while expecting their personal sacrifice to mean as much to anyone as it does them.

The same goes for your *Me Time*. If you don't value your time and make others acknowledge its importance, you are sending a message that it is open for someone to take from you. While emergencies may arise, poor planning on someone else's part does not constitute an emergency on your part. Show others you value your time. Taking regular *Me Time* sends others a clear message that you love yourself and you value your time. When others see that you place value on your time, they will likely see it as valuable and be less inclined to think you have nothing better to do than to serve their needs.

Finding the Formula

It would be great if I could give you a magic incantation that creates *Me Time*. Truth is, anything worth having takes work...or at least thought.

Think about this: **Planning +Time Management + Permission = Me Time**

Making It Work for You

By now, you may be wondering how you will find the time to take your regular *Me Time*. Life is crazy and busy and there will be days you will want it and it will be impossible to get it. That's just life. It's like dieting (except now we call it "practicing a healthy lifestyle". You have to plan ahead and be determined to stick to it. If you falter, you don't keep faltering. You go right back to following your plan. Therefore, in order to be successful at capturing your *Me Time,* you need to look carefully at your typical day and plan carefully. I suggest you start by asking yourself the following questions:

How efficient are you at using your time wisely?

What can you do to rearrange the elements of your day to create a block of *Me Time?*

Do you have a network of trust-worthy parents you can swap and share babysitting times with?

What resources are available for child care that fit your individual needs?

What kinds of activities are eating up your day?

There are many free or inexpensive ways to get the guilt-free time you need for yourself. In today's economy, every dollar counts. If you find you need to shell out a few bucks, rearrange how you spend your extra cash, or make a small sacrifice to get your regular *Me Time,* consider it an investment in your health. If it involves physical exercise, then you're getting even more bang for your buck. The returns may very well make a big difference in your life, health, and relationships.

Permission to Be Selfish

When my oldest child was very young, her biological father asked me this: If you and she were stranded in a remote area and it was a couple days hike back to civilization and you had just enough food for one, what would you do - feed her or eat the food yourself? Of course I said feed her. She's my baby. Apparently, that was the wrong answer. He pointed out that I would be no good to either of us if I just fed her because I would need the energy to get us both to safety. The choice would be extreme but ultimately we both would be better off. I hated the thoughts of such. I wasn't sure why, but that question burned in my belly for almost 20 years before I was ready to embrace the full meaning of it. I finally resolved that God allows seeds to be planted and when we're ready that seed produces fruit we can use. At that point in my life, I couldn't imagine ever putting my needs before my child's, so the analogy was lost on me. I was seeing the scenario too literally. I was unaware that everything, including selfishness, has a place. It's up to our human judgment to decide to which degree to use it.

...for the Single Parent

Selfishness serves two purposes: survival and choice. One is primal. It keeps the human species in existence. The other separates us from other life forms because of human judgment. Just for kicks, let's start with survival. Animals in the wild survive by taking care of their own needs first. Even birds get theirs first before they take food to the nest. Mother bird is of no use to her babies if she starves to death trying to fly back and forth attending to their needs. I'm not literally talking about starving anyone here. Don't get me wrong. Feed your family, please. But feed your own needs too... *all of them*. Give yourself the daily bread of life that is given to you. It's all there, like a gift. Personally, I believe our Creator meets all of our daily needs. What we do with our time and resources determine how our needs are met. Accept it all and choose wisely...with your best judgment. As for the second, selfishness and judgment go hand-in-hand. Selfishness is perfectly acceptable but you judge to what degree you apply it to your time.

So how does one decide it's okay to be selfish enough to set aside regular time for just yourself? In the words of one of my good friends, "give yourself permission". I love those words of wisdom. (Thank you Mark Wiggins for writing <u>Permission to Succeed</u>.) I took Mark's principle of giving oneself permission to succeed and applied it to giving myself permission to be selfish. It wasn't easy. I needed to be in a better place, mentally and physically. One was the result of the other. I had to step outside my comfort zone and give myself permission to do what I needed, to be successful...and to fail. I've busted my ass on my journey but I'm in control of the elements of my life more than ever. Can YOU give yourself permission to be selfish *enough* to take the *Me Time* you need to reach your goals?

The Snowball Effect

I mentioned earlier in this chapter that not only are the effects of taking your *Me Time* cumulative but the effects may spill into other parts of your life. Improving your mental and emotional health has been known to increase performance and efficiency in working and learning. At home, you may find you are more pleasant, more patient, more likely to accomplish overwhelming tasks you dreaded or procrastinated before. Your better mood may become contagious to your children. You may see physical changes as well, especially if you use your *Me Time* to do some stress-relieving, physical activities which could lead to losing a few pounds, improving your appearance, and hopefully improving your health. Additionally, this could boost your self-confidence... and that looks sexy on anyone. This alone is a great motivator to become more active. See where this is going?

Consciously doing one simple *action* to improve your life can snowball into positive effects for you and your loved ones. I love the changes I am making in my life because of the *Me Time* I regularly take. I am more empowered, more confident, and feel better than I have in many years. I feel like I have more control over the elements of my life and my elemental self is thriving.

By-the-way, MY Me Time, is usually taken in a gym. I initially lost 40 pounds and lowered my cholesterol and blood pressure. Additionally, I've recently taken that a step further with clean, organic eating and am controlling the quality of food I serve my children. I am healthier than I have been in years and no longer need the prescription meds I used to take for anxiety and depression. I empowered myself to lose other toxic nonsense and clutter in my life, including leaving an unhealthy living arrangement. Now I'm thriving in my new, independent life.

Give yourself wonderful gifts too. Love yourself. Love your children. And love the special people in your life, by allowing yourself to be selfish enough to take your *Me Time*. Nurture your elemental self. Then watch your life bear amazing fruits of peace, improved health, and accomplishment.

Dr. Kreslyn Kelley-Ellis

Life experienced first, then, academically trained - Educator, Entrepreneur, Trainer, Mentor, Coach, Community Servant and Activist.

Kreslyn left the field of education, to start her own business, Premier Leadership Academy. Her passion is still educating children, but now also includes educating adults. Her platform has moved beyond the school house, to conference rooms, auditoriums, and office space. Her subject matter has changed from reading, writing and arithmetic to leadership, diversity, character building, team building, goal setting, and helping others identify individual purpose and passion. Dr. Kelley-Ellis' ultimate goal, is always to help anyone seeking higher ground realize that it is not only possible, but it is inevitable! Her simple, yet dynamic approach is making herself real and transparent to others by sharing her own stories of challenges and triumphs. She is one of the featured authors of the book, *My Vision, My Plan, My NOW!*; *My Now for the Entrepreneur;* and *My Now for the College Grad..*

For more information, visit her site, **kreslynkelley.com** or **placademy.net**.

...for the Single Parent

Taking the Sin out of SINGLE
Dr. Kreslyn Kelley-Ellis

I remember the day he enrolled, James, a cute little kindergartner with the widest grin and curliest hair for all to see. His mother, Sarah, was so softly spoken, kind, and as pristine as could be. My secretary got James registered and ready to go, and then walked him to his new classroom. His teacher smiled, welcomed, and introduced him to all of his classmates. They were warm and inviting, and some of the little girls reached to touch those beautiful locks in his hair, which were as long as theirs. It was a great day, right? But, of course!!! In fact, it was a great week! However, not much longer after that week, we discovered we had some serious challenges with James, his Mommy, and his Daddy, that would last us for years to come.

You see, James' Dad had been imprisoned and was now a free man again and back in his life. Mom and Dad were no longer together and had not been for quite some time. James, as it turns out, was very angry, defiant, disrespectful, and sometimes all out violent. I conferred with Mom countless times by phone, numerous times in person, and I even got the opportunity to meet and dialogue with dad a couple times as well. As the principal of this school with a few hundred students and as parent of my own three children, I was very empathetic to the apparent issues they were facing while trying to rear this child between two different households with two different set of rules (neither very structured). Therefore, I did everything I could to mediate between the two, support and educate the child, and provide a safe and disciplined environment for James as well as for all the students.

It was apparent to me that they both loved their child and that they were doing the best they could do, though their actions weren't necessarily best for the child. Mom made apology after apology to him, me, and his teachers about James being bounced between two single parent households, as if that was something foreign to us or something in which she should be ashamed. Both of them made too many excuses to even count for his behavior. They implemented numerous tactics to appease him, like buying him the newest sneakers and other lavish gifts, in which he would just come to school and brag about while teasing other students who did not have such luxuries.

James was suspended several times and brought to my office almost weekly throughout his intermediate years. We put interventions in place, like time with the school counselor, time with a mentor, one-on-one tutoring to help him when he'd miss time in the classroom, due to the excessive amount of times he could not be there because of his total disruption of the learning

...for the Single Parent

environment. I know James' case is somewhat extreme, but I witnessed many children during my career as an educator who where in similar situations; single parent home, parents that felt guilty about the fact that things did not work out between them and the other parent, parents bickering and blaming back and forth in front of the child, and parents appeasing a child's behavior versus getting that child and perhaps the parents themselves the help they all needed. Simply put, parents can sometimes unknowingly and unintentionally get so wrapped up in "self" and worry so much about how they appear to others that they totally overlook the real issues and the impact these matters are having on the child. This is not always a single parent issue either. Single, married, divorced, traditional or nontraditional relationships, I think we've all been guilty at some point in making apologies and carrying the burden of guilt and shame about a "perceived" mistake we'd made pertaining to our relationship, marital status, and rearing our children.

Think about it. How many times have you walked through the park, the mall, the grocery store, anywhere, and you found yourself in a conversation about why you are parenting alone as if it warranted an explanation. I am amazed at how we accept the negative stigma placed on us by society, because we check off that box, which is labeled ☑ Single, ☑ Divorced, or some other category, which may not seem ideal. It is what it is; and, it is NOT a sin to have been in an unsuccessful relationship. It is not a sin to have joint custody or primary custody or your child. It is not a sin that you chose to raise your child alone, because you know it is the best thing to do for him, her, or them. It is not a sin to choose being alone versus dating, nor is it a sin to have the courage show up to church, parties, weddings, and other events alone. Point blank, it is not a sin to be Single!!! Therefore, an explanation of your singleness and your single parenting does not permit a requested or unrequested explanation. It is simply okay to respond to that standard question, "Oh, what happened?" with a gentle and smiling response like, "Nothing" or "Life happened".

According to Kids Count Data Center, a project of the Annie E. Casey Foundation, 35% of America's children are in a single parent home in 2012. That is 24,725,000 children. I say that to say this, "you are not alone!" Now, let me be clear about where I stand. I am not a proponent of children growing up without fathers and/or mothers, but what I am an advocate of is raising children in healthy and loving families; and, sometimes that does not happen in a two-parent home. Also, I know that if a parent feels guilty or ashamed of being a single parent then those negative feelings can be passed on to the children, leaving them to feel like they are to blame for their situation, when they are not. Also, I am a champion of people who are determined to rise, daily, and give life and parenting their very best. Life without children is difficult enough; and, adding family dynamics only magnifies the complexity of living, striving, and thriving. Therefore, someone's marital status and household status should not be a factor to someone else's resolution as to whether something is wrong with them or not.

As a former unwed single parent of two, divorcee, then single parent of three (in that order), I personally felt the brunt of others' judgment, criticism, and all out disrespect at times. It can be the most humiliating circumstance when a person who has never been a single parent either question your status; or, even when you watch television shows, movies, world news, and other forms of media and entertainment and all you see is single parent home depicted as impoverished, at-risk, hopeless, and tragedy prone. Another deflating feeling is when you live in a very religious culture and the apparent upright show unnecessary pity to a single parent family, demean a young single mother who may lack some essential tools for parenting, or cast a sense of despair upon being single, being a parent, and the chances of finding a mate to compliment your family. Notice, I said, "compliment" not "complete". Our aim should always be to be complete and whole as individuals, not halves looking for another half person to complete us. In fact, I've discovered that looking for someone to complete your family is sometimes a response to the guilt one feels for leaving the child's/children's father or mother in the first place or even to simply help out and ease the relief of the financial burden single parenting can cause.

Other overcompensation plans for single parenting can include making excuses for children's wrongful behavior, defending them no matter what, not creating or enforcing solid and consistent discipline plans at home; but, the one I think is most prevalent is renting our children. You may be thinking, "Now what do you mean by that?" Well let's define renting. To rent to pay money for the use of something that does not belong to you. So, we often pay for items that: 1) are unaffordable for us 2) the children may not have earned or even sometimes deserve 3) children did not request... just to make us feel better about the perceived sin of parenting alone. The shame is not yours to spend money on. It is the unhealthy perception that has been transferred to you by others and/or that you conjured on your own and is now being passed down as gifts to your children.

Let me also state that that spending excessive amounts of money and/or money you don't have on your children is not just an issue for some single parents, but there are many two-parent households that do the same thing. This kind of behavior has also been linked with "spoiling" or "overindulging" children, probably because if the parents give, exceedingly, in the areas of finances, it is likely the child gets what he/she wants in many other areas as well, even when it is not rightfully earned or even necessary. Some parents, who cannot afford to give lofty financial rewards can be just as guilty as well when they give greatly and unnecessarily in other areas, because the premise is the same: overcompensation! The danger in this is that the world doesn't operate in the same manner. When your child goes to school, he will only be awarded for appropriate and good behavior. When your child goes to college, she will be given an A when she earns it. When your child goes to work, they will be compensated based on the salary scale, hourly wage, and amount of hours one works, and there will be no exceptions, even if he wants new shoes or need additional money for a weekend at the beach. Therefore, overindulgence may feel good to you in the moment when it stops your child from whining or being mad at you; but, in the long run, it can set your child up for failure.

It is completely human for us to want to give our children the world, and it's normal to sometimes not know the boundaries between healthy provision, rewarding, and spoiling. No parent is perfect, and as caregivers we must make provisions for our children; however, it's pertinent that we do within our means. It is equally vital to reward them with the gifts and possessions they want "occasionally" and when they've earned them. Moreover, it is just as important to provide them with healthy thinking about decision making even when some of the decisions they might have to make in life are not popular or may cause them temporary pain. It is valuable to teach our children that occasionally we all make mistakes or sometimes we do what's best for us and it may not seem that it's best for others; but, we don't have to live in regret, guilt, shame, condemnation and embarrassment over that decision, and we don't have to live a life of self-martyring trying to repay those who've stated that we've hurt them. We do not want to pass on the "renting" mentality to our children and have them continuously look for ways to pay people a debt they cannot afford and compensation in which they were never liable.

In the event that you've already employed such practices in your parenting it will, no doubt, be challenging to change. In fact, the longer you've carried the load of sin or renting, the more the difficult it will be; but, it's not impossible. Some of the most critical areas families often neglect is the need for intervention when attempting to modify such behavior. Family counseling, spiritual intercession, coaching, and professional guidance can be beneficial paths where this behavior is deeply embedded in one's psyche, especially for those who experienced such behavior for generations. These chains are never broken without the recognition of the behavior and the intention to change it. You know the saying, "If you always do what you've always done, you'll always get what you've always gotten." Here's another one, by Einstein, "Insanity: Doing the same things over and over and expecting different results." If we know that this behavior doesn't help us with effectively raising the kind of children we want, then we must not continue with it.

At the end of day, most parents want the very best for their children, though we may parent in different ways, the way that we know based on how own personalities, cultural backgrounds, life experiences, religious beliefs, etc. However, there are some basic guidelines that everyone can follow when trying to raise a child to be healthy and whole individual, a productive citizen in society, and one that will bring you pride and joy in your old age. So, if you love your child(ren), give your **HEARTT**! Here's how...Those things include, but are not limited to...

H - Healthy Home: Children need an environment where they receive all the elements they need to be healthy physically (balanced diet, exercise, water, safety, security, and discipline to include rewards and consequences)

E - Enjoyment. Children need the opportunity to sense love in their hearts, feel it with arms around them, hear with words that speak love to them and encourage them. They need to be able to play, laugh, and indulge in sports and healthy hobbies. And, under no circumstance should they be held responsible for adult issues in which they lack understanding and the maturity to handle.

A - Acceptance. All children are uniquely made, having their very own DNA. Their difference should be celebrated and cultivated; and, they should never be compared to siblings and other children.

R - Reading: All children need to be exposed to different reading materials to stretch their minds beyond what is in their immediate surroundings. They need to be culturally aware and sensitive to people who are not like them. They need to learn about heroes, philanthropist, and spiritual leaders who've made a difference in society. They should read sacred passages and writings which demonstrate right living and higher thinking. They need to be able to see pictures of other parts of the world and learn some of the facts pertaining to those places. This type of reading will stretch their minds, prick their hearts, and give them much in which to aspire.

T – Truth: All children need to have open and honest dialogue with people they trust. They need family time to safely discuss rules, expectations, desires, and disappointments. This communication should be ongoing. Great communicators establish great relationships, and they are also great writers.

T – Time: Finally, YOUR TIME IS THE MOST VALUABLE THING YOU CAN GIVE YOUR CHID, NOT MONEY & THINGS!

Have fun being a single parent. It's a gift and a blessing to have children and it's a great opportunity to mold them the way you want them to be. It may seem like a struggle, but the situation could always be worse, whether you are alone or with someone. So, relax, enjoy the journey and every time you are tempted to buy in order to pacify your child, take that money and put it into a college fund! If you give them your HEARTT, you no longer have to pay rent on something that doesn't belong to you: guilt and shame. Your children will be happier and so will you!

...for the Single Parent

My Now...

Natasha Jeter

Natasha Jeter is the proud mother of one, and a self-proclaimed "Jack of all trades, Master of a few." She is a graduate of Broad Run High School c/o of 2004, and has her Bachelor of Science Degree in Political Science and African American Studies from Old Dominion University.

A member of Delta Sigma Theta Sorority, Incorporated, Natasha is a force to be reckoned with in the community, serving as an Official Election Officer, and a Trustee on both the Black History Committee and local Museum Board.

For bookings, you may email jeternatasha@gmail.com or follow her on Facebook: Natasha Jeter.

...for the Single Parent

Learn to Invest in Your Child's Success
Natasha Jeter

"The potential possibilities of any child are the most intriguing and stimulating in all creation."-Ray Lyman Wilbur, third President of Stanford University

"Dorothy is turnin' over in her grave right now because you don't have your son!"

"Why? He is a boy, and he is with his Father-what's wrong with that?"

"Yeah, but he should be with you! But you wanna travel all over the world and whatnot!"

As I let the misguided words of my eldest Aunt linger in the air, and question if my beloved Grandmother would disapprove, I questioned myself; why does it matter? The world has become entirely too comfortable with the idea of a single black woman raising her child, while the father is only permitted visitation. What she meant to tell me was that it would be more comfortable to *her* if I were to raise my son by myself full-time, as opposed to successfully co-parenting with his father-a damn good one at that. When did this become the norm?

Yes, *I do* want to travel the world; I have a natural zeal for life along with ambition and talents I yearn to share. Yes, *I am* a single woman, but never have I considered myself a "single mother"; that would be taking away credit from his father which is undeserved. Finally, yes, *I do* have a precious gem of a son who spends a large amount of time living with his father. Why? Because that is what we agreed upon, and if anyone else has an opinion about it, they are more than welcome to express themselves while simultaneously paying for his seasonal wardrobe, year-long swimming lessons, video games, annual sports team participation fees and respective uniforms for soccer, football, baseball, and basketball, his impending piano lessons, foreign language classes, and the bottomless pounds of food- specifically fresh fruits- that a growing boy such as he consumes. If it is more convenient, I will immediately set up a PayPal account for them to contribute to his 529 Savings Plan.

Now that I am done allowing those to whom the previous section was referring take their seats, let me begin my parental anecdote by emphasizing this: my son's father and I REIGN at co-parenting, and really practice investing in our son's success. It all began seven years ago…

...for the Single Parent

Thursday, December 6, 2006 3:23am

"It's a BOY!"

Well thank GOD, because that's who we had been preparing for these past nine months anyway! An impressive 7 pound 14 ounce, 21.5 inch long bundle, my son, Quincy James was born out of what our elders call "young love". Almost four hours southeast from home, his father and I were both enrolled in college that semester, and had even made the Dean's List. The first child for us both, aside from the doctors and nurses, we were the only ones in the hospital. His family knew, while mine did not. When I left the hospital two days later and started to receive birthday calls from friends and family, true to my unconventional "dance to the beat of my own drum" fashion, I casually let them know...

"YOU WHAT??! Why didn't you tell anyone??!" my cousin accused.

"I wanted to simply take responsibility and have a stress-free pregnancy-free from anyone's opinions or thoughts," I replied calmly.

"What are you going to do about school?" my mom asked fearfully.

"We are both still enrolled and on the Dean's List. We came up with alternating schedules so that someone is always

My Now...

home watching Quincy and we don't have to worry about daycare."

"I knew it-I dreamt it!" my unconditionally loving grandmother smiled through the phone.

According to plan, it was exactly how I wanted it to be. Here we were- two young kids away from home, enrolled in school part-time, working part-time, and not a single family member in the area. We considered ourselves grown and were acting as such, so call home for what? Now, don't get me wrong, my son's paternal Grandmother was *indeed* instrumental in us securing our home and extremely supportive. She was very much so our saving grace and my son, whom we affectionately call Q, adores her dearly. While it wasn't traditional by any means, Q's father and I took full accountability for our blessing of a situation without interference from anyone else. I know now, that it was actually the best decision we could have made because I grew up alongside him, and into the woman that I am today. Despite things not working out between us, he and I do phenomenally well by making sure of one thing: we remain heavily, personally invested in our son.

Now, when I say personally invested, I mean being the main catalyst to their growth. We taught our son any and everything we could and to make sure education was consistently at the forefront. Quincy had picked up a pencil and began "serious scribbling" at ten months and looking intently at picture books. I read to him-just as my mother did to me nightly-as often as I could. Now he reads a new chapter book each week of his own volition, and is extremely articulate in his manner of speaking. Honestly, there was no particular format that we followed; we did what we *felt* we should be doing. We fed him string beans and carrots as if they were candy and watched all the cheesy educational television programs with him interactively, to instill an early love of learning. Looking back on it now, it was an undeniable advantage to have still been college students when first raising our son. I was even a tutor at a local elementary school and made sure to memorize the curriculum and manner in which the young students were taught so I could take it back home to share with my son.

I put Q on the computer at the tender age of 2, and though he initially broke a few of the keys on his father's brand new Mac laptop, I was able to focus him on using a few key buttons to play a pre-school alphabet game which he thoroughly loved. Today he is able to manage and utilize his own email account which I help oversee. It's also no wonder he loves video games and desires to create his own one day! Imagine my amazement when at 6 years old I found him on my laptop navigating YouTube—yikes!

"Quincy, what in the world are you doing on my laptop?" I asked nervously.

My Now...

> "Excuse me, Mama, but I am trying to figure out how to beat this level in Luigi Mansion", he replied innocently.

> "Wow, and who taught you how to do that?" I challenged him. He looked up with a wide-spread grin and responded, "You did, Mama!"

Here I was thinking to myself, I did?? Not unh...wait, perhaps I did! You would be surprised how much we forget we actually teach our children, and how well they pay attention and absorb information- even when we think they are not mature enough to comprehend.

At the end of the day, all of these examples can adequately affirm that both of Q's parents love him to infinity and beyond. We both led very active campus lives and successfully graduated college—baby boy and all. Whether a single parent, or part of a co-parenting situation, one should *never* be too busy to learn how to invest in their child's success. My sister works with children every single day of the week, is a college student, and yet still finds the time to look up fun science projects to experiment with my nephew—who isn't even two years old yet!

I also feel like you are never too young or old to do right by your child. While I am still growing wiser each day in my role as a mother, I'm looking ahead eagerly knowing, that the best reward of parenting will be seeing the effort, sacrifice, and tender loving care invested in Quincy come to fruition. I can hardly wait! #ProudMom

...for the Single Parent

Part 3: World's Greatest

My Now...

Pamela Glowski

Pamela Glowski resides in Northeast Ohio and is currently a CTA Certified Life and Human Capital Business Coach as well as the owner of Serene Insights, LLC.

Pamela's purpose is to assist all of her clients, as their "Change Coach", while they work from transition to transformation, and achieve new found success and results. After solidifying her own success, she chose once again to follow her entrepreneurial spirit and launched Serene Insights in late January of 2014.

Pamela's first entrepreneurial venture came within the travel industry in 2005. She had developed proven strategies and had earned a position as a trainer and featured speaker in several Direct Sales Events including webinars, conference calls and live appearances.

Pamela is a CTA Certified Coach in both Life/Business Coaching as well as Human Capital Coaching. Her years of education and experience in working with all types of individuals and companies has allowed her to gain insights that enable her to create and use powerful coaching techniques, accountability steps and true compassion to allow her clients to "Create The Life You Can't Wait To Live"!!

If you would like to learn more about Serene Insights and Coaching with Pamela contact her directly at Pamela@sereneinsightscoaching.com. You can also visit her website at www.sereneinsightscoaching.com

We Can't Be Married… But Let's Be Good Parents
Pamela Glowski

I don't think that I ever had a heavier heart than when my ex-husband and I came to the conclusion that our marriage had reached the point of being irreparable. There was too much hurt, and the looming truth that we had grown into two completely different people than when we had gotten married had been realized. In my heart I know that I was the one who had made the most significant changes. And it was I who had asked for the divorce. I knew with that one decision, every part of life as we knew it was going to change. We were going to move forward single again, not as a couple or as a family unit. I was going to have my life and he was going to have his. Our parent's lives were going to change, our work lives were going to change, our friends were going to change, and most importantly, our children's lives were going to change, and they had no say so in it. When we told them that Mommy and Daddy weren't going to be living in the same house anymore, and that they would be living with both of us, they didn't really understand. It became very obvious, as the tears started to flow, that they were confused, sad, and very unsure as to what this announcement really meant for them and life as they once knew it. Knowing this I said to my now ex-husband, "We Can't Be Married…But Let's Be Good Parents".

I don't believe that anyone goes into a marriage with the intention of ending up divorced. No one wants to be a statistic. According to Divorce.com, under an article they have posted entitled, "Divorce Rate", "since the 1970's, marriages have declined 30%. Divorce is up 40%. Over 40% of first marriages end within 13 years. 20% fail in the first 5 years. Of those divorced, 75% will remarry. 65% of second marriages fail. Premarital Cohabitation is up 70% since the 70's, with 50% of these relationships failing in the first 5 years. For those marriages where premarital cohabitation preceded marriage, 50% failed". The numbers are staggering. And in many of these divorces are children of all ages.

My children were 6 and 3 when we separated and divorced. I am not a believer in staying together "for the sake of the children". I believe that children, if in a home where their parents are committed to each other, should see a loving relationship. They should see the parents working together to build their home and loving each other as a foundation for the home. If there is a "loveless" marriage, I think this type of union is even worse than living apart and being good parents in two separate homes. I believe it is possible to work together, as partners to raise the children, even though the two parents live in separate homes.

...for the Single Parent

Many will disagree with my opinion, and I accept that. I base my opinion on having watched friends of mine, who had parents that were married, but really lead separate lives. The children had no example of what marriage, or the core of what "real" marriage was about. Or at least what I believed it was about. In some cases I had seen parents that weren't even nice to each other. They communicated with each other on a very limited basis. I wasn't going to live in a way, that in my opinion, made a mockery of marriage for the sake of racking up years. If I was going to be married, I wanted my children to see how successful marriages run on a daily basis, working through disagreements, hugging each other in the kitchen, making decisions regarding finances with everyone's best interest at heart. I wanted my children to know marriage was sacred, and if I wasn't going to live, the examples of love, friendship, and honor, in my own marriage, then I didn't want to mislead them.

I have very deep rooted beliefs about marriage. I was raised in a Catholic home and believe me, my decision to get a divorce was not well received. I had been taught that a husband loves his wife like Christ loved the church and a woman was to serve her husband. I believe that when two people decide to get married, they have built this type of commitment through God, their chemistry, the friendship that they have with each other, mutual goals, same belief systems, and a true connection with that other person. Every marriage goes through ups and downs and there are times, when those feelings are tested. But, in the long run, with the right nurturing and attention, they get back on a level path if they start to wander. I don't know of any marriage that doesn't endure hardships, doesn't have challenges or doesn't get pushed to the limits. I have to admit, in my pursuit of goals, dreams, and personal success, I was largely to blame for not paying attention to my marriage. Before I knew it, what we had in common and what we had built our relationship on was no longer the same, and there was not the same connection.

I don't think that I ever felt more thrust into being a responsible "grown up" than when I had made the decision, the papers were inked, and it was official. I was now a single parent. I had lived on my own, had my own place and ran my own household before I had gotten married, but then it was just me that I was responsible for. Now I had to make sure me, and two little ones were taken care of. I actually had done it before because my ex-husband and I had worked separate shifts. Me on first, he on second. But when he would come home, if I needed help getting the kids dressed, fed or off to day care he was there to help. Now, I had to make sure I had everyone all ready to go with everything we needed for the day, no safety nets.

One thing that became apparent to me very early on was, **if I was going to keep my promise to be a good parent, I had to take care of myself**. If I wanted to be able to take care of them to the best of my ability, I had to take care of me. I kept with my exercise routine that I had developed over the year prior to my divorce and let my kids know that it was important for Mommy to keep it up. They had grown used to coming down in the morning and sitting on the couch while Billy Blanks walked me through Tai Bo at 6am.

I had to make sure that I was eating right. I prepared meals in advance so that when we came home we would have a meal. I would only allow us to have fast-food one time per week. Not only for health reasons but budget reasons. I only had one income now and I had to take care of me, by taking care of my finances too.

The last area that I felt was critical, was my emotional health. The emotions were a whirl wind. There were days that I was angry at me. Days I was angry at my ex-husband. Days I was angry at family and friends. Though I understood that they were struggling with their own emotions, some of the things said to and about me were hurtful. There were days that I had felt that I had made the worst decision of my life, but the bridge had been burned. I felt guilty for what I had done to my ex, and for what I had done to my children. Then there were the days that I felt so free and happy that I was living on my own. It was a true roller coaster. I had to pay very close attention because it just seemed to swing back and forth. I was exhausted just from the emotions and knew that I had a lot to work through.

Fortunately, I had a great network of friends and family who I was able to talk to, but not many of them had ever been divorced or had been a single parent. At times during our conversations, many of them grew uncomfortable and most of them truly didn't know what to say. I did have a few friends who had been there and for their insights I was so grateful. In addition I did a lot of reading of books, researching resources online, and listening to radio talk shows. I tried to tune into any resource that would be helpful. **I didn't feel that I needed to see a psychologist to work through my emotions, but I do believe that for some people, it is a resource that should be used if one is finding it difficult to deal with their own emotions. I also think it's a critical resource if one is finding it difficult to deal with their former spouse and parenting partner in a healthy way.**

Part of being a good parent was learning the ground rules for each other and agreeing to what was going to be acceptable in our environments in raising the children. Of course we didn't always agree. I was always more rigid about bedtimes, what to eat before bed, and movies they watched. Their dad was always the fun one anyway and had a more relaxed approach. It was easier when we lived together to hold them to the schedules. I had to learn early on that what he decided his rules were going to be in his house were his rules. If he let them stay up an extra 30 minutes, I needed to stay out of it. My ex-husband was always a good dad to the kids. I never had to worry about safety issues or neglect. If that is an issue one finds themselves facing, I would enlist the help of the proper authorities. For the sake of this chapter, I am focusing on what I call "highly functioning" parenting partners. Parents who are very conscious about their actions for the sake of the children.

Many times I have seen divorce situations where the parents use the children to get back at the other parent. If you find yourself tempted to let your emotions interfere with their relationship, with their other parent…STOP…STOP NOW!! **I was told very early on to NEVER talk badly about, tell children stories about the other parent, or do anything to try to make that other parent look bad…It will backfire on you EVERY TIME. I believe this to be the best advice that anyone ever gave me.** I call it the "Boomerang Theory". Whatever you throw out, can, and will, come back at you with equal speed and force. You will be the one to end up looking bad and cause your children to distrust YOU. That's not being a good parent. Accept the fact that you may have divorced the person, but your children have divorced NO ONE. They love both of their parents and no matter what the reason you have ended up divorced, it has nothing to do with your children. They have to be given permission, by both parents, to love their other parent, and to have their own relationship with them. You also have to accept the fact that even though you are divorced, because you share children, you will always have a tie to that other person. If you had divorced before you had children, you both could have just walked away and never had to see each other ever again. Whether you were married, lived together or just had children together, understand, once there are children, you are forever bound. There will be reasons like school events, sporting events, graduations, weddings…that you will have to be in the same room with that other parent. How those meetings go, can go one of two ways, and really how it goes, is completely dependent upon each of you.

I never had more reinforcement of this than when my little girl was making her First Communion. At this point I was remarried. My ex and I had established a good parenting relationship and we decided that for her party, we would all celebrate together. I invited all my ex-husband's family, all of my current husband's family and my family. We probably had about 75 people on her special day. At one point during the party as I was stirring spaghetti sauce over the stove, my daughter ran up to me, grabbed me around the waist and said, "Mommy, I'm so happy!"

I said, "Why honey, because you made your First Communion?"

She said, **"No Mommy, because everyone that I love is here…in one place!"**

I had tears well up in my eyes because even though we were long past the divorce, the aftermath still affected my children in everything they did. Who would they see? When would they see them? Was it Wednesday, the day to go to Dads? Whose weekend was it?

One day, when my son was feeling frustrated with the traveling between two houses, said, "When do we get to have a say in when we go? Maybe I would rather go on Thursday rather than Wednesday? We never get a say!"

That was when I decided that they could go whenever they wanted as long as they had arranged it with their Dad. Because it wasn't fair. For years they went back and forth, and back and forth, and no one asked them if that was in their plan for the day. This has worked out nicely through the years and it also helped my relationship with their dad. He knows I would never stand in the way of their relationship.

As the parents of your children, you have to be secure in the relationship you each have with your children. If you are so concerned that they are going to love the other parent more than you, your insecurity will be what drives a wedge between you and that child, not the other parent. If your insecurity finds you being downright destructive to the other parent, in the end, it's only going to hurt you. It may even land you back in court. It may affect your visitation or how often your children want to be with you. If your former spouse is the one being destructive, ask to have a meeting with that parent to talk about this and make them aware that your intentions are not to come between them and the children. You may have to be the bigger person until they see that you are not going to hurt their relationship.

You will find that communication with the other parent becomes essential. Yes, essential, if you truly want to be a good parent. **You may find yourself talking more to your former spouse just because you both need to keep each other updated regarding the children.** You may be saying, really??? Whether you are the residential parent, or not, whenever anything comes up regarding the children, either from teachers, coaches, doctors, their friend's parents, etc., you have to relay it to the other parent. When my children were younger, I made sure that I shared all school calendars, fliers, and correspondence from teachers so that we both knew what was going on with the children's school lives and extracurricular activities. I also shared when I may be out of town if it wasn't my weekend. This is a good thing to do especially as you start having teenagers. No parties at my house! As the children form friendships, you will also have to be very honest with the other parent regarding your experiences with their friends. It wouldn't be the first time that kids conduct themselves one way at your house, and then push the limits at the other parent's house.

Now you may be saying, **"I can't talk to my former spouse"**. Find a way. If you really want to do the best for your children, find a way! I have seen divorces that were like "The War of the Roses" with children involved and unfortunately, the kids were the ones who suffered. No one wants to see their kids end up in therapy, so why not take the initiative, even if it means the two of you, or the entire family, get a family counselor, to help you provide the best communication to support your kids.

As I said before, it's important to set up ground rules, or maybe a better term for it would be your Adult Code of Conduct. Most of what I have described above is more about you and how you interact with your former spouse than it is about rigid rules for the children. No parent should be giving the other parent a list of rules for them or for the children. The courts handle those guidelines. If one parent tries to control the other, that isn't going to work either. We don't have control over any other human being. This goes back to making sure that you are keeping your own emotions in check when dealing with your ex. **Whatever structure you would like to establish should be talked about respectfully and agreed upon mutually. Be open to the other person's points of view, LISTEN, and decide what is going to be in the best interest of the children.**

I know that you might be rolling your eyes as you are reading this, thinking there is no way that you could ever get to that level of communication with your former spouse and co-parent your children happily. I'm not saying it's always easy. There were many challenges, many times we made two steps forward, then fell two steps back. We kept at it because we made that promise to ourselves and to our children; we kept working at it. It's been 14 years since my divorce and I have to say, because we gutted it out, and found a way, my children are well adjusted. We succeeded. They love all of their parents, grandparents and are thriving.

My ex-husband and I, together with his wonderful wife and my fantastic husband, in the most recent years, sat together at football games, laughed and had great "catch-up sessions" as we took photos for homecoming, and have saved seats for each other at graduations.

It can be done. If you are committed to those you love the most…YOUR CHILDREN…and they are worth it.

Keep your promise and remember, **"We Can't Be Married…But WE CAN be Good Parents."**

...for the Single Parent

My Now...

Mark W. Wiggins

Mark "The Speaker Man" Wiggins, an International speaker, trainer, author and entrepreneur is the CEO of Xtreme Effort Speaking. He has held leadership and management positions within several national retail companies, such as Foot Locker, Eddie Bauer, and Levi Strauss & Co. He has trained corporate, community, and association leaders in the Washington, DC area on the topics of customers, leadership and human performance.

He is the author of *Permission to Succeed: the Only Person Who Needs to Give it is You*; *MTXE the Formula for Success*; and more. He is also one of the featured authors of the book, *My Vision, My Plan, My NOW!*

Get my information right now! Text the word "Speakerman" to 90210.

Email: Mark@markthespeakerman.com
Tweet: @Speakerman87

Divorced... But Still a Dad
Mark Wiggins

Man Up

Once, a divorced friend of mine had to "snatch his son up". (Translation: he had to have a man to man with his teenage son.) His son had disobeyed and disrespected his mother - he came at his mother like he wanted to hit her. Later, the mother called the father and told him what had happened. My friend told his son's mother, "No worries. I'll take care of it."

That day, the father picked his son up from school and had a pivotal conversation with his son. He made it perfectly clear, to his son, that the behavior he displayed and disrespect he showed his mother was completely unacceptable. Although my friend did not live in the house, he made his son understand that if it happened again, he would approach him like a man and deal with him "accordingly". Some may think this harsh, but if my divorced friend had still been living in the household with the son and mother, he would have been expected to handle that situation the exact same way. Needless to say, the young man got the message loud and clear. Mission accomplished! This divorced dad was able to step into *his fatherly role in his child's life, effectively handle his business, and still maintain his living status outside of the mother's home.*

My Fellow Single Dads,

You may no longer be a husband...but you will always be a father.

The focus of this chapter is to communicate that although you are divorced from the person with whom you have children, you have not been released from your responsibility to your children. Expectations from society of divorced and single men has discouraged us from being around our children because we are too often labeled as "broken" and "unfit" to raise our children. Being a dad is tough. There may be times you secretly wish to leave all of the drama and hassle behind and move forward with your own life. Of course you can't skip out; you divorced your wife, not your kids.

Even as a single dad, living in another home, I know that there are lessons to teach, hearts to mind, pivotal conversations to have with my son or daughter, and pitfalls of youth to guide my children around. *My kids need me to be present and accounted for. So does yours.* By present, I mean be a known commodity. Your children should know if they call or need something, Dad will be actively attempting to do his best to make it happen. All the while, be willing to provide your knowledge, as a man, to teach

...for the Single Parent

life's lessons. Your perspective is not that of their mother. Children need that "balance" to be able to see life from multiple points-of-view, as their lives unfold. You love your children. One of the best ways to show that is to "be there" for your children. I have met many fathers who have found themselves in situations where they may not be fully present in the physical lives of the children; however, these men were still able to do a helluva job as strong, effective, and loving fathers.

Crime and Punishment

A very close friend of mine had to deal with a situation that was just devastating. He and his wife split in a bitter divorce but his daughter remained "his heart". The mom took the daughter and left the state, then made it next to impossible for him to honor his commitments of visitation to his daughter. What did he do? He did what he could to visit, call, write letters, send texts and emails, etc. He did what he could to make sure his daughter knew she had a father. Sometime he would fly out to see his daughter on his visitation time, get there, and the mom would make the child unavailable. WHAT?! She used their child as a pawn in her game of crime and punishment. It was hard to watch but he never gave up. As his daughter got older, she began to appreciate her father's efforts and began demanding that she see her father. Now that she is of legal age, she can see her father whenever she wants. Just think... what if my friend had given up on staying in contact with his daughter when the mother was making his visitation next to impossible?

Trying to get a parent-child relationship started later in life is a game of chance. It just might not happen. You have to do your part (and sometimes more), even if it makes your ex upset to have to deal with your visitation. Past issues aside, at the end of the day, your children are what is important and you are still their father. If you continue to be the dad your children need you to be, even during the tough times, the times will come when you will be called upon to do *only* what a father can do. When that time arrives, you need to make sure that your child knows, without a shadow of a doubt, that you are the father that they need you to be. Just because your circumstances limit your role, it does *not* mean your effort has to be limited as well.

Sage Advice

While you still may be working through the aftermath of your divorce, there is help out there for single fathers who feel overwhelmed by their changing parental circumstances. Find a support group. Surround yourself with others who can share great advice and counsel...and talk you "off the ledge" from time to time. The following advice are some pieces of wisdom that I have gathered along my single dad journey. Feel free to add to this list and empower more men, who are divorced or single to be the father their children need. In fact, if you have some tips to share, email or tweet me (see bio for contact info).

...for the Single Parent

Be present.

Show up as much as you can be with your children for events, birthdays, and other special occasions. Kids may not remember each visit but they will remember that dad is always "there for" their events. Just showing up can make a big impression on a kid. If you can, occasionally be there when there is nothing special going on. Perhaps you can call to see if you can get more visitation time. Approach your ex by offering to give her an occasional break. (Approach this with caution because some exes can take unfair advantage of this kind of offer.) Additionally, you may want to arrange to join your child at school for lunch or after school, at the library, to help them study.

I make it a regular practice that when my child calls, to stop everything, if I can, and take that call or answer that question. Of course, I advise you to set boundaries with your children on how this system works or this could possibly backfire on you at work...or in a special social situation. I also make it a practice to inform the women I date, before we go out, that if my children call, I *will* be taking that call. There is no discussion; my children are that important. My children know that dad is always available for them. Actions speak volumes and go a long way toward creating that trust and security, even when I am not physically there with them. What kid doesn't take comfort in knowing that their dad always has their back?

My Now...

> Remember it's not always about you.

This is a tough one. Sometimes you will have to work with your children's mother to get things done, for the sake of your children. Regardless of the personal issues between you and your ex, keep in mind that it's *not* about either of you anymore. Your marriage and intimate relationship is over. Co-parenting is about the issues and commitments *to your kids*. Set down with your ex and have a kid-focused, adult conversation. Create an understanding and communicate how children-related issues will be handled. Committing to this mind-set *should* keep everyone's attitude in check.

Also, remember that your children are watching you both. How you each handle awkward or tough situations in life sets the example your children will follow when they face a conflict in a relationship. Deal in grace and take the high road. The behavior that you both model in front of them will shape how they deal with their relationships later in life. Additionally, be ready and willing to admit your short-comings and learn to apologize to your kids for what you said or how you acted when you fell short of acceptable expectations. This lets them know that you are human and you will fail. Make it clear to your kids that this is how people should reconcile their differences and repair broken friendships and relationships. Teaching humility is more than talk - it's an action.

...for the Single Parent

Spend time... not money.

It's easy to spend cash but it takes sacrifice to spend time. Time cannot be recovered. Money usually can. Therefore, time is more valuable. Fight the feeling that you have to buy everything your child's sees or wants just to gain their approval or make them happy. These are feelings, not tangible goods. It's tough because you want them to have fun. But be careful of "guilt purchases". Buying things because you want to make up for not being there or to appease an upset child (or co-parent) sends the wrong message. This does not help your kids set real expectations of relationships and sets them up for more disappointment when you cannot consistently live up to that type of unrealistic, gift-giving standard. Remember, it's the time you spend with them they will remember, not the stuff with which you bought off your guilty conscience.

Communicate often.

Do what you can to communicate with your kids, even if sometimes it's just one way. They'll know that you're thinking of them. Send the text, the tweet, the post. Call. Put a card or letter in the mail, just because... as well as for special occasions. These are *all* forms of communication. More importantly, they are signs of love. Share your thoughts and dreams that you have for your children with them. Let them know that you think about them, pray for them, and are concerned about them. Let them know that there is nothing too big or bad that they cannot tell you. When they are ready, they will come to you because they will know you will listen to them. However, you have to take the lead and set the example. Sometimes, they may not like that you call so much but they'll notice if you don't.

Keep the kids out of it.

Never use your kids as emotional pawns in the battles between you and your ex. It's tough when they say, "Mom said" or "Dad said" to the other parent. It's too quick and too easy to reply with, "Well you can tell them...it's not their business...and another thing...." Learn the art of "the exhale". When you get those words that make your hair stand up, EXHALE... and say, "Ok, well... I will talk to your mother about this."

Keep the grown up stuff, grown up and the kid stuff, kid stuff. Most kids really care less who does what, as long as it gets done. Please understand that how kids are dealt with during these times is how they will deal with people in their relationships because kids will often imitate what they see. Keep them out of the lines of fire if you and your ex have disagreements. Let them be kids - not messengers that get shot when they come baring bad news.

Move Forward

Living outside of the same home as your child is tough. You may feel as though you are on the outside and out of control of how they are being raised. I've shared a few things you can do to start becoming a more involved father in your child's life. If you have not started this yet, don't waste time and energy regretting it. Forgive yourself for wasted time and begin where you are today. In my book, *Permission to Succeed*, I talk about how you are the only person who needs to give you permission, to move forward, to reach your goals. Read this excerpt below about how you can forgive yourself for the time you have wasted:

Have "that" conversation with yourself.

Figure out just why you're not allowing yourself to move forward. Be open and honest with yourself. Holding back the truth will not help YOU in this conversation. You must be brutally honest with yourself.

Stop pressing the rewind button.

Reliving the emotions of the past is not a great way to move forward. Remember, the mental energy needed to recreate that level of emotion can build barriers that hold you back. Stop reliving and start knocking those barriers down. Use the crumbled stones of that wall to build steps to your healing and become the Dad you were created to be.

Begin where you are.

You cannot go back in time and recreate the past. Even if you must start from scratch again, you have more knowledge than you had before. You are already better off than you were back then. If you have not done the best job of being a divorced or single father, start today. There doesn't have to be a meeting, report, or even permission from anyone else but you. Just decide *how* you want to be better and do it from that moment forward. "A journey of a thousand miles begins under one's own feet." You have to think and want the change, to start the process of changing for the better.

Silence the whispers.

Shut down that self-doubt talk and move forward. The whispers are just another mechanism to hinder you from moving on with your life that can even hinder you from reaching your goals. Acknowledge those whispers. Deal with them, then move forward with your plans to be the kind of father you have always wanted to be.

As a divorced father who doesn't live full-time with my kids, I still grapple with the emotions and issues concerned with raising my children; however, by doing my part and being consistent in my efforts (while remembering that someone is watching), I remain a stable influence and active participant in their lives. Please understand it has not been easy, I have struggled through *everything* I have written about in this chapter. Perhaps you see single fathers that may make it look easy, but our choices are never easy. Our hearts are always divided, when living apart from our children. I encourage you to use my advice to keep you from becoming an "outsider" in your children's lives.

Even with All My Flaws

I am always amazed when my kids remind me of things they remember I said, way back when. Things like: the woman walks on the inside, away from the street; the man should always keep the tickets for movies and shows; always remember mother's day and your sister's birthday... so many others my father passed along to me. As a man, I feel I must live by example the lessons that I was taught and expected to pass on to my children. It's a subtle legacy from my father to my son; a silent expectation from my mother to my daughter.

One of the most impactful moments I have had, as a [divorced] father that continues to encourage me to make sure I stay actively involved in my kids' lives, was when my daughter told me, "Dad, when I grow up, I want to marry a man like you!"

"Even with all my flaws and the mistakes I make?" I asked her.

"Yes," she replied, "because you've shown me what a man is supposed to be like - good times... and bad...and that he is supposed to provide and protect me. Dad, you have never let me down."

At that moment, I was holding back tears but shouting on the inside. I told her, "Well, it may be tough, but one day you will find that man."

That being said, I have to also make sure that my son becomes "that" man as well - for his future family. A mother can teach her son many, wonderful things, but a father is the only one who can mold his son into a man.

We have a mission to do, fellow fathers. We can never give up. We may stumble but we cannot allow ourselves to fail. Stay vigilant. Keep up the good work, take control of your parental role, and remember...YOU CONTROL HOW YOUR LEGACY IS BEING CREATED RIGHT NOW.

Sincerely,

Divorced, But Still a Dad

...for the Single Parent

Tina L. Collazo

Tina L. Collazo is a mother, poet, writer, speaker, and entrepreneur. Over the past 5 years, single parents have sought out her wisdom about how to have success in their life spiritually, mentally, emotionally, physically, relationally, and financially.

Tina has written a devotional called "Virgin to The Mic" filled with uplifting and inspiring poems as a result of her journey as a divorcee and single mom. She serves as a Life Group Leader for Single Mothers and Separated/Divorced Women as well as an AWANA Leader for the First Graders. Tina has been invited as a guest speaker at local high schools to talk about Marketing, Business Office Environment, and launching "Success for Teens, Teens Using the Slight Edge".

Tina is a mother of two awesome boys, J.C. and Nicolaus. She is a successful Real Estate Agent and Investor, and specializes in the Northern Virginia market.

Email: tina@tinacollazo.com
Website: www.TinaCollazo.com
Twitter: @TinaCollazo

...for the Single Parent

Show Unconditional Love
Tina L. Collazo

As a single parent, it's important to show your children unconditional love. The love they need from you money can't buy. An iPhone, Xbox, or any other techy gadget isn't going to do it either. You have to show them love with hugs, kisses, words of Affirmation, and with your actions. Also, it's when you interact with them and show your emotions towards them. Over the past seven years as a single mom, I've come to master unconditional love with my two sons.

For example, I've found that words of Affirmation have really been huge for my kids. Kids need encouragement too and kind words can go a long way in life. I was sharing with a friend about how I speak life into my children in this way. I told her that I would have to say to my oldest son, J.C., when he was struggling with math that he is a champion, he is smart, and he is a winner. I would have him repeat what I said so he can internalize it. He would get so mad at me and mumble through it. J.C. didn't believe he was those things. Even though there was no evidence of that yet, I knew deep down he was and he would become who he said he was in due time. Every day we worked hard on his math work and it was like working out, no pain no gain. There were moments I wanted to quit myself, but I kept reminding him every day about who he was. One day, the light bulb went off and he finally understood how to solve the math problems. That day he said on his own, "Mommy, I'm a champion. I'm so smart!" He believed in himself finally and embraced being what I declared over his life weeks before. As a parent, I have to plant those seeds because one day I won't be there when he's away at college or when life happens, and he'll have to encourage himself with his own words of Affirmation.

There are times out of the blue when I just say to my kids individually, "Hey, come here. I think you're a great kid and that you're awesome!" It's so unexpected and random. They always look everywhere else but in my eyes when I say that because they are not sure if they are ready to receive that compliment. I tell them to look me in my eyes and I say it again to make sure they get it.

Funny enough, one day my kids, J.C. and Nic, who are 9 and 8 years old surprised me with that same gift. Their words of Affirmation to me were "You're a great mom." They said it individually and I knew they meant it. What made it even better is that J.C. looked me in my eyes when he said it. Nic chimed in to agree with what his brother said. I didn't ask for a compliment nor did I expect it. I knew at that moment they were really happy with me, and that I've done well creating a consistent and stable home environment for them. Their world was right and they wanted me to know that. It was a Proverbs 31 moment for me. My children rose up and called me blessed!

Another example of unconditional love is showing your kids how much you care. Last November, I had to make the decision to pull my children out of the after school program they were in all together. Before then I used to pick them up by 6PM and go over their homework with them while I cooked dinner. Typically, I would find their homework was incomplete or incorrect when it was done at the afterschool program. Also, their paperwork would be disheveled from them going through it and I couldn't figure out what should stay home and what should go back to school. To top it off, the communication between their father and I was a challenge since we did not communicate about upcoming tests, projects, or homework. I decided something had to change to ensure their academic success.

In moving forward with our new routine in November, I created a schedule from getting home and unwinding, to having their afternoon snack, to homework time, and playtime. The first few weeks were hard because we had to get into a rhythm and I had to figure out their learning style to effectively reinforce what they were doing at school. It was very empowering to see their work daily, successfully prepare for tests, and get their projects and reports completed on time. I am so thankful I'm self-employed and was able to modify my schedule for my children.

I put my faith in God and trusted Him to work out all the details. As a result, Quarter 2 has been a huge success. I was able to show my children how I love them. I'm home when they get home. I ask them how their day was and what they learned. They talk to me! They share their world and include me now in the things they really like. I also realized how much I needed to see them every day during the week and that I felt robbed as a mom for years on the days I didn't see them. Also, I enjoy making them afterschool snacks and meals when they are really hungry. I love being a mom and am really blessed that God is giving me the opportunity to show them how much I love them through my actions. What I'm doing everyday tells them that they are important to me.

Another example to consider in showing unconditional love is the human touch. I'm an affectionate mother. I hug and kiss my kids as much as I can. I want them to feel my love for them. The morning and night seem to be the most intimate moments with my children. J.C. would never be seen in public hugging and kissing me let alone walking with me because he's so independent. However, on weekends when they are with me he's the first to get up in the morning and come into my bedroom. I smell his stinky breath as he nestles himself under my chin. I want to say go brush your teeth, but I know that's the last thing on his mind and he's taking advantage of the one-on-one intimate time with mommy. At that moment he doesn't have to share me with his younger brother, and he loves every minute of it. Funny enough, my youngest son will take the kisses and hugs all day and in public. In fact, he'll push his cheek towards my lips and crawl into my lap like I'm his chair.

Something special my mom used to do would be rubbing my head and back, and stroking my hair when I was a kid. I would fall out every time. I will admit that even as an adult, I will lay on her lap when I visit her and she still plays with my hair. It puts me to sleep every time. It has a calming effect and it's love to me. As mom, I do the same thing to my kids. At night J.C. and Nic ask, "Mommy, can you rub my back?" I have done this with them since they were babies. They love to be touched by me whether I rub their backs or massage their heads. At the end of the day to them, it's mommy love!

A few other things I do to show unconditional love are to allow my children to express themselves in their interest and not judge them. My oldest, J.C., likes to break dance, and sing loud and out of tune. It drives my youngest son, Nic, crazy! He politely tells his brother to be quiet. Sometimes it doesn't work. I just laugh because I need J.C. to be comfortable in his own skin and build self-confidence by doing the things he enjoys that's positive. Nic loves dogs and carries around his stuffed lab named Chocolate when he's at home. He consults with Chocolate about things that he's unsure about or not ready to give a direct answer on. Chocolate seems to be his security blanket. In the next year or two, I'm sure he'll grow out of it. I respect where he's at as he's trying to figure his world out that is ever changing as he experiences new things in his life.

In summary, remember to hug and kiss your kids as much as you can. Ask them what they are thinking about, what they liked best about something, and how their day was. Use words of Affirmation like "you're so smart," "you are a champion," "you are a great kid," and so on. Speak life into them to build their self-worth because you are shaping them into who they will become. Spend quality time with them and make it count! Don't focus on the quantity of time basing it on the number of hours or days you are with them. You have to work hard to be fully engaged and in the moment because they can tell. Unconditional love looks like going to Chuck E. Cheese with your 8 year old or drinking a latte at the mall while you people watch with your teenager because that's what they love to do. It's also about being there, supporting their interests, and not judging them. When they know you love them, they know you have their back.

...for the Single Parent

Sharon A. Myers

Sharon A. Myers is the Founder and Executive Director of Moovin4ward Presentations, a youth empowerment company that facilitates character building, leadership and success workshops for high school and college students, as well as at-risk youth around the country. She is also the co-developer of the youth program, **Journey to Success: Personal Success Strategic Plan (PSSP) Program**, which is based on the book *Mapping Your Journey to Success: Six Steps for Personal Planning.*

Sharon is also the author of *Slumber Party* and *Are You Talking to Me;* and is also a contributing author in *My Vision, My Plan, My Now, My Now for the Entrepreneur,* and *My Now for the College Grad.*

sharon@moovin4ward.com
www.Moovin4ward.com
www.Journey2Success.com
Tweet @moovin4ward

...for the Single Parent

Full Sun for Balance

Sharon A. Myers

I learned in elementary school that plants grow toward the light; and if that light is only received on one side of the plant, the plant will lean in that direction towards that light. If the light were moved to the opposite side of the plant, the plant would eventually, within a day or so, sway in the opposite direction. If the plant received light on both sides, full sun, it would grow straight up... balanced.

With more than 50 trees in my backyard, I've noticed that the same applies to trees. If a tree only receives the morning sun with a building or other trees blocking the afternoon sun, it would grow leaning towards the east. That east side of the tree would grow healthy and full of thriving green leaves and new branches, while the other side would have fewer limbs, less foliage and brown or grey in color.

However, a tree growing in open field, tends to grow straight up with a near perfect, rounded shape, full of healthy limbs and leaves on all sides because it receives the *full sun* on all sides.

In my opinion, like trees and plants, kids need full sun for balance to grow straight and well rounded.

The full sun that I'm speaking of is the balance that comes from two parents, whether they are married, never married, or divorced. Kids naturally long for stability and steadiness—an equilibrium, which is a mental, physical, and emotional balance between influences. Even when these influences come from their sometimes very different, divorced or unmarried parents.

Opposites Attract

So let's take a few steps back... before the baby was conceived. Now I realize that there are always exceptions to the rules, but I'm going to put this rule out there anyway. Opposites attract. Sure, when you meet someone and are attracted to them, you have to have something in common. But at the same time, and usually unknowingly, it's the differences that pull couples together.

But to be clear, I'm not talking about differences of how you wash dishes or your favorite pizza toppings. I'm talking about personalities, temperaments, and behaviors. For example, if one enjoys talking and social gatherings, the other enjoys peace and quiet with cozy intimate time. Or if one enjoys strictly following rules, procedures, and plans, the other likes to play it by ear, stay flexible, and be creative.

...for the Single Parent

While dating, those differences may be barely noticeable and somewhat attractive. For example, a male that is loud and boisterous will typically be attracted to the quiet, reserve female. Or the introverted, cautious male is attracted to the outspoken, aggressive female. Or a woman that tends to be frazzled and hectic is attracted to the tidy and organized male.

I honestly believe that we unconsciously choose potential mates that are strong in the areas where we are weak. However, when the two marry, the differences tend to become more obvious and stand out like a sore thumb. When one is faithfully trying to save money and the other is constantly spending it, it becomes a problem. Whenever I have a friend that complains about a characteristic of their spouse, I always ask, "Was he/she like that when you dated?" Nine times out of ten, the answer is yes. It's not something new, it was there all along, but ignored. Those differences work to keep some couples married for life; for others, not so much.

It's like the Yin and Yang of life. Yin and Yang describes how opposite or contrary forces are interconnected and interdependent in the natural world and how they give rise to each other as they interrelate to one another. Day versus Night. Cold versus Hot. Love versus Hate. Life versus Death. We need both for perfect harmony—balance.

Then comes the baby. You have a couple of things at play here. First, that baby is either a girl or a boy. No brainer. Both genders require a balancing act when it comes to parenting. Boys and girls have different needs that must be supported. Second, that boy or girl will have its own personality. I'm told that a child's personality is developed by the time they reach three years old. Having four kids of my own, I can certainly vouch for this theory. I can also vouch for the fact that the child's gender has nothing to do with their personality. I have two girls who are nothing alike and two boys who are nothing alike. And to be completely open and honest, all four of them are very different. But each personality and gender will require a balancing act of parenting. Let's discuss both.

Balance for Personalities

Remember, in most cases, the parents are very different. So we may have a "play first, work later, fun parent" and a "work first, play later not-so-fun parent." This sounds like a bad thing, but it's not. It offers the child balance. It becomes important in the development of the child. Too much of one without the other is not good for anyone; especially if it's opposite of the child's personality and doesn't foster growth.

Kids need a parent to teach self-control, enforce discipline and establish rules. But they also need a parent to teach us to have fun, try something new, and enjoy the blessings of life. I venture to say that we need a parent to connect with... someone who truly "gets us." Someone who enjoys the same things we enjoy and understand what truly motivates us and why we value it. It means a lot to a child to have that "likeness" with a parent; they brag about it.

But when there is only one parent in the home and that parent is very different and struggles to understand what drives the child, there will be difficult times ahead without that connection. Thus the equilibrium of the child is off. Now if your child is fortunate enough to have full or equal access to both parents, the differences are less traumatic. And don't get me wrong, I'm not saying that a child can't survive and grow up to be a productive citizen with one parent... because I came out okay. I'm just saying that the balance is off. Trees with sun on one side still grow; albeit a bit lopsided.

When I was a single mom, I only had one child, a son. With the addition of three more kids, I quickly learned that I couldn't parent them all the same, because their personalities were so different. While one (or two) may need more stringent punishment for bad behavior, such as spankings, yellings, or timeouts; others might only need to see the disappointed expression on my face to exhibit their best behavior. They are different, have different needs, and require different negative and positive reinforcements.

If you are the fun parent and are caring for the fun child... that's almost awesome. You'll have a great time, but you might lack the ability to show your child structure and discipline and/or confuse your child when you flip back and forth. That's not to say that you can't do it, but it won't be natural for you. And it might even hurt you to enforce the rules. But if you don't, you might have too much fun and lose control of your child.

The same applies when you are the strict enforcer of discipline and rules caring for the kid who loves structure, boundaries and rules; it's almost awesome. But someone needs to introduce "fun" to your child. Someone needs to introduce "change and spontaneity" to your child. Otherwise, they risk not developing social or healthy emotional skills.

My first two kids enjoyed fun and flexibility. Clean rooms, homework, or going to bed on time were not high priorities for them. Truth be told... those were not high priorities for me either. Yes, I know these are important, but I never really got bent out of shape about them. They needed their father to be the enforcer of these rules and to teach the importance of establishing self-discipline and order. It doesn't mean that I couldn't teach those things, but I had to remind and force myself to stay on them about it.

My younger two kids prefer structure and plans. These two have a hard time accepting change, experimenting with the unknown, or doing things on a whim. There is only one way to do anything and that's the right way from a plan or checklist. They fear doing anything wrong and therefore run from risk. This works for their father since "change, unknown, and whim" aren't part of his structure most of the time. So I spend a lot of time trying to push them to try something new, have more fun, and be more social.

They all need balance. They need light on all sides to grow straight, tall and well-rounded within their personalities.

Balance for Genders

Based on my experience with my four kids and the many kids that I have ministered to at my church, I've decided that a child's personality has nothing to do with gender. Kids need a balance in this area as well. Obviously, girls need their mothers or a mother-figure for physical and emotional support. For the same reason, boys need their father or a father-figure.

A girl's physical and emotional development is something that only a woman can fully understand. That's not to say a good father couldn't do research, ask questions, read books, and learn the physical changes; but he'll never be able to fully grasp the changes and/or be able to provide factual experiences of his own to relate. In fact, trying to understand or fake it might even drive him insane… without some female guidance.

And let's not overlook the physical changes that a boy undergoes. When my oldest son became a teenager, he was running through soap and lotion like nobody's business. I swore he was drinking them or something. I was clueless. Interestingly enough, all the men in our lives knew EXACTLY what was going on. They didn't clue me in right away, but assured me that he was healthy and not drinking soap and lotion.

When my youngest son came home from middle school with a puberty pamphlet, he blew past me to his father to share what he'd learned about his body. Frustrated, I wanted into the conversation. I convinced him that I had a son before him and I had a younger brother; so anything he could share with his father, he could share with me because I'm well aware of boys and puberty. So my then 11 year old son reluctantly asked, "Are you sure?" I nodded. He then said, "ooookaaay," and handed me the pamphlet. I flipped through the pages in excitement that I would have to opportunity to participate in the important discussion. Then, I came across the word, "erection" on one page and "ejaculation" on another. I handed him back the pamphlet, told him to talk to his father, and walked out. Not for me.

But gender balance is more than just the physical development of the child. It also includes the emotional development and understanding of the opposite gender.

...for the Single Parent

When my oldest son wanted to talk about girls, he came to his mother. When he was ready to purchase a Christmas or Valentine gift for a girl, he again relied on his mother for help. The first (second and third) time that a girl broke his heart, he came to his mother. He needed to understand why and only felt his mother had insight into a girl's mind. While it takes a father to raise a son from boy to man; it takes a mother to teach the son how to treat, love, and respect women.

Just like a girl needs her mother to teach her how to love and respect herself; she needs her father to *show her* how to be treated, loved and respected by a man. Her relationship with her father is significant in how she navigates her future relationships with potential mates. If a daughter is accustomed to being treated badly by her father and/or watched her mother being treated cruelly by him, she may believe that this is normal and end up in an abnormal, dysfunctional relationship.

The same applies with boys and their mothers. As a teen, I was told that I could learn a lot about the type of person my male suitors were by their relationships with their mothers. If he had a healthy and loving relationship with her, he'd know how to treat me. If he treated her badly and/or disrespected her, he'd treat me even worse.

Balance.

My Now...

Full Sun

To grow up mentally, physically and emotionally strong, kids need sun on all sides. Don't spend too much time trying to fight the fact that the other parent is "doing too much" differently than you would. The child doesn't need two of *you*, he or she needs a mixture of two parenting styles to provide balance.

If the other parent is not available or not willing to be a light, there are other options. Kids of single parents with large family support systems do very well. I relied greatly on my church family, where men were more than willing to take my son under their wing and provide that male guidance. Later my husband stepped into the slot. There are also other options such as The Boys and Girls Club or Big Brothers/Big Sisters that are helpful.

Look for opportunities to give your child the balance he or she needs to grow up straight and well rounded. This includes pushing for opportunities that the other parent can shine on him or her as well.

So whether you have a son or a daughter, and whether your child's personality is just like yours or completely the opposite; ensure they get full sun on all sides for balance.

...for the Single Parent

My Now...

Kevin E. Boston-Hill

Kevin E. Boston-Hill is the consummate educator. He has been an educator at many levels in New York for over 18 years. He has conducted professional development workshops for his staff, families and others in many areas including instructional technology and 21st century learning. His profession gives him instant motivational opportunities, as he is a sought after speaker and emcee, having spoken to thousands of students from around the country.

As a member of Kappa Alpha Psi Fraternity, Inc., Kevin serves as the Northeastern Province (Regional) Guide Right Director. He coordinates activities, trainings, and conferences for all of the guide right programs and directors from Rhode Island to Delaware.

Kevin is also a voice actor and has recorded several audio and video projects that were used for professional development and training purposes. Kevin uses his experiences as an official in baseball/softball, basketball, and volleyball to further connect with and motivate the people he comes in contact with.

You can follow Kevin on Twitter (@kbhspeaks)

LinkedIn (www.linkedin.com/kbhspeaks)

...for the Single Parent

School on Your Time, Not Theirs
Kevin E. Boston-Hill

"I want to leave my children and grandchildren with a mentality that says, 'I can fight to get a piece of the American pie'." - Dorothy Brunson, American broadcasting executive

As a parent, single or otherwise, the primary responsibility is to raise our children to believe that they can accomplish anything. Along the way, we place an emphasis on obtaining an education and developing a strong sense of independence. These tasks become increasingly hard for the single parent who has to single-handedly provide all of the basic necessities. While this may seem like a daunting task, there is hope.

One of the biggest concerns I get from parents is that while they understand the importance of education and want their student to do well, but they just do not understand the new curriculum and can't help their student when they run into difficulty at home. Let me tell you - it is okay. Now you need to tell yourself that it is okay that you do not understand the work your student receives. Teachers don't expect parents to completely understand the curriculum - especially the math! Admittedly, the standards and curricula change so frequently in many states and school districts that it is often difficult for teachers to keep up. Add to the lack of knowledge the fact that you frequently work long hours or even multiple jobs and you may ask, "What can I realistically do to support my child?" The following tips should help and are effective at any grade level:

Create a special place for homework. While you may not be able to always complete homework assignments with your child, you can still reinforce the importance of homework by setting aside an area for him to complete assignments. Pick a place that has good lighting and free of interruptions. If you have limited space, cord off an area (even if you have to put tape on the floor to separate a small area) that will serve as the homework spot. Remind other people in the house that when someone is in the homework spot, the noise levels and distractions have to be kept as low as possible. This will instill the importance of homework in your children and teach them to be considerate of others. Allow your child to decorate the area and maintain a stock of supplies (pens, pencils, paper, folders, etc.) to develop responsibility.

Understand the teacher's expectations. Check in periodically with your child's teachers so you are clear on homework expectations. When and how are test dates communicated? Are study guides provided? When are assignments like book reports and special projects due? Are assignments to be typed or handwritten? You can request your child's teachers to provide weekly progress reports or send you updates periodically. Most teachers utilize technology a great deal and have set up classroom websites where homework is posted daily as well as other information.

Develop a homework routine. Students become very busy with after school activities so it becomes increasingly important to establish a set time to work on homework upon getting home and stick to it. We are all creatures of habit, and our students are no different. Once students see that you are serious about supporting their homework habit, it will become easier for them to maintain. Even encourage others in the house (including yourself) to do homework, pick up a book or newspaper, or do some other household chores. The key is to have your child see that everyone has work to do, not just her, so while she is doing something that is not all that fun, no one else is either.

Encourage use of a planner. The old Day Runner is a thing of the past, but students of all ages should get into the habit of writing things down in an actual paper planner. This way you can also check their assignments when you get the opportunity. Older students may want to utilize their smartphones or other electronic devices, but stick with the paper so you can have unobstructed access. Besides, many schools provide their students with planners at the beginning of the school year. Ask your school if they do and if not, maybe the PTA or PA will be willing to subsidize the cost.

Anytime is a good time to review. One of the most powerful questions you can ask your child is, "What did you learn today?" Don't let your child off the hook with the standard, "Not much" or "Nothing really" or "The usual stuff" or any similar response. This is when you find not only what your child is learning, but you discover any difficulties he may be having academically or otherwise. Use the time you have together to review concepts. Household chores can be used as opportunities to reinforce math learning - measurement in cooking, calculating and adding tips when dining out, calculating sales and tax percentages while shopping (if these can be done in her head, even better).

Help students set goals. Many students procrastinate (and I bet that includes the one(s) in your house) because they feel overwhelmed by the assignment that they were given. Show them how to divide the project into smaller steps - marking daily or weekly deadlines in the aforementioned planner. Doing a little bit each day will make the task seem more manageable.

Another concern that parents often have is about testing. They know how important tests are (classroom as well as state exams), but they also know how nervous and anxious their students get on test day. Check their attendance patterns or when they call home complaining of headache or nausea. I am willing to bet that many of those are the same days that tests are given. Many of us are not good test takers (as evidenced by some of our SAT scores, but I won't get into that), but we can alleviate the anxiety in our children. Here are some do's and don'ts to think about regarding test anxiety that should be explored from the beginning of the school year:

DO tell your child that there will be occasional tests. Classroom and standardized tests are how a student's performance is measured, therefore it becomes a necessity. However, the preparation is key to exam performance. As long as students are utilizing the planners and keeping up with their assignments, they should feel prepared for any test that is put in front of them.

DO make sure your child attends school regularly. Encourage traveling with a buddy. When students become responsible for someone else, they rise to the occasion and attendance rates improve. Attendance is important so students don't fall behind, increasing the anxiety related to test preparation.

DON'T get upset because of a single test score. I know we want our students to score high on every test, but there are many factors to consider for a low score: illness, lack of concentration, little sleep the night before, family concerns, or even boyfriend/girlfriend problems. Think about how many tests and assignments you messed up because of the cute guy or girl who broke your heart.

DON'T be shy about meeting with your child's teachers to discuss progress. Meetings do not have to be face-to-face, they can be via email, phone, or text. Determine the best mode of communication for you during your work schedule and relay that information to your child's teachers.

DO make sure your child receives healthy food before a test. Foods heavy in carbs or sugar will lead to feeling groggy or hyper, which will make it difficult to concentrate. Something simple like a bowl of oatmeal and fresh fruit would be a healthy choice.

DO NOT UNDER ANY CIRCUMSTANCE ENCOURAGE CRAMMING. You may have felt that it was necessary to read 6 chapters the night before the big history test, but that will most likely increase test anxiety in your child and interfere with clear thinking. However, if the proper preparation has been followed, cramming will not be necessary and he can get a good night's sleep before the test.

It is understandable that single parents are busy and can't always show up to every meeting or event. Determine your best mode of communication and relay that information to your child's school. Many teachers will set up appointments before or after school on days when you can't make the designated Parent-Teacher Conference days. Maintain contact via email and ask for progress reports and information flyers to be sent this way (though I am sure you receive all of the handouts that your child receives, right?). It is important that you develop a cooperative relationship with your child's teachers and not an adversarial one. You can even be proactive and ask the school to offer workshops and programs that would be of interest to you in helping in your daily activities. Show them that you are willing to compromise on meeting, but they should be able to work with you. After all, it is the academic, social/emotional, and physical success of the student we have in the balance. If you and the school cannot reach an accord, it is inevitably the child who suffers.

One such parent workshop that you may want to suggest is increasing internet and social media knowledge. While most students stick to the mainstream social media sites like Facebook, Twitter, and Instagram, there are a host of other social media apps that exist and more to come. There may be no way to keep up with all of them, but you should be aware of how they work and how the privacy settings are controlled. It is vitally important that you have conversations with your student around being safe on the internet. Even if you feel intimidated by a lack of internet or social media knowledge, the power of parental influence is strong. You have to teach them how to use the internet responsibly, including discussing the digital footprint. Students need to understand that everything they put on the internet can be seen by millions, if not tens or hundreds of millions of people and has a longevity that will outlast them. All of their online searches are tracked and stored so online companies can develop profiles on them. Just remember that while your child may be more digitally experienced than you, his lack of life experience can quickly get him in trouble when it comes to social media.

Here are some important tips you can use to keep your child safe on the internet and social media:

Require your child to accept you as a "friend" or allow you to "follow" so you can see who else is part of her social media circle.

Insist on knowing your child's account password. This is a non-negotiable.

Monitor online behavior and if you see any post you deem as inappropriate or dangerous, (any post that has personal information such as address or phone number, any status that announces where they are or if they are alone) have your child take it down immediately and explain why.

Explain that they should not post anything that they would not say in person or that would embarrass them if grandma read it. (More on this in a bit.)

Do not use Reply All if the response is meant only for the sender.

With the expanded use of the internet and social media have come increased incidents of bullying, cyber-bullying, and sexting. Because students can hide behind a screen name and avatar, they feel emboldened to make inappropriate comments and disparaging remarks aimed at other people. The news is filled with stories of students who have not wanted to attend school or even killed themselves because of the incessant remarks and responses on social media. Just as disturbing is the rise in the number of sexually explicit content that students send to each other, whether in words or pictures. What students don't realize is that once a picture or text is sent to another person, it can, and most likely will, be sent to a whole host of other people that were not intended to receive the message. In addition, there are legal implications to sexting: people can be charged with pornography for sending, forwarding, and even receiving sexually explicit messages. If the image is of an underage person, child pornography laws may apply. This may be a difficult conversation to have, especially for the single mom to her son, or single dad to his daughter, but it is necessary. The internet can be a very adult place.

You may be wondering what can you do if it is your child who is being cyber-bullied. More than likely, the victim of cyber-bullying is also being bullied in person. Have a conversation with your child's teachers and administrators to see if they have noticed any change in behavior. Monitor even more closely your child's online interactions. Ironically, those who are being cyber-bullied actually engage in more online chatting, texting, and posting - all in an effort to win over the crowd. What the victims don't realize is that they are only making matters worse - usually providing the bullies more ammunition for continued bullying behavior. When cyber-bullying is suspected, immediately remove your child from the situation by shutting down computers and mobile devices. Copy and save the malicious texts and posts and bring them to the school administration to arrange a meeting with the bullying student's parents.

Of course, the internet and electronic devices are constantly changing and as mentioned earlier, sites that are popular among teens pop up almost daily. The best way to stay abreast of the changes is to simply talk to your child. There are plenty of opportunities - while preparing dinner, traveling to the mall, sitting in the barbershop or hair salon - that you can take advantage of to ask any of the following questions:

Which are your favorite sites to visit?

What are your favorite activities to do offline?

What would you do if someone you met online asked to meet you face-to-face?

Besides me, who do you feel you can talk to if you are faced with a scary or uncomfortable situation? By the way, if you are NOT a person he feels comfortable talking to, this is a good conversation to have as well.

How do you decide who to add as a "friend"?

What kinds of things do you post?

Does anyone else have access to your account passwords?

Have you ever regretted anything you posted online?

What information do you think is okay to share online? What information should be kept private? Why?

Now that many schools are incorporating electronic devices into their learning, including becoming 1-to-1 (one laptop or tablet for each student) or BYOD (Bring Your Own Device) sites, it is important to inquire about their "Acceptable Media and Internet Usage" policies and agreements and ask for a copy to review with your child at home.

Always remember that as parent, you are the first line of defense when it comes to your child's education and development. It is understandable that you will be busy and your availability may be minimal, but the same tools that are used to update your status or to follow your favorite entertainer can be used to stay in constant communication with your child and his teachers. Schools may exist to serve students and their families, but parents need to provide the parameters by which schools can work cooperatively with them. This means making sure phone numbers and email addresses are accurate so everyone can make sure our students get what they need to be successful.

...for the Single Parent

Books by Moovin4ward Publishing

My Now for the College Grad:
Motivation to Succeed After College

By Moovin4ward Authors

My Now for the Entrepreneur:
Motivation to Start Your Own Business

By Moovin4ward Authors

My Vision, My Plan, MY NOW:
Motivation You Need to Take the Action You Want

By Moovin4ward Authors

My Now…

Mapping Your Journey to Success: Six
Strategies for Personal Success

*By Sharon A. Myers &
Mark W. Wiggins*

To book a certified Moovin4ward speaker to present a program, email speakers@moovin4ward.com

To purchase any Moovin4ward books in bulk (20+) at discounted rates, email books@moovin4ward.com.

www.Moovin4ward.com or www.Journey2SuccessPSSP.com.

www.ingramcontent.com/pod-product-compliance
Lightning Source LLC
Chambersburg PA
CBHW060514090426
42735CB00011B/2214